T0285036

not thinking like a liberal

not
thinking like a **liberal**

Raymond Geuss

THE BELKNAP PRESS *of* **HARVARD UNIVERSITY PRESS**

Cambridge, Massachusetts | London, England   2022

First printing

Library of Congress Cataloging-in-Publication Data

Names: Geuss, Raymond, author.

Title: Not thinking like a liberal / Raymond Geuss.

Description: Cambridge, Massachusetts : The Belknap Press of Harvard University Press, 2022. | Includes bibliographical references and index.

Identifiers: LCCN 2021034389 | ISBN 9780674270343 (cloth)

Subjects: LCSH: Wolff, Robert Paul. | Morgenbesser, Sidney, 1921–2004. | Cumming, Robert Denoon, 1916–2004. | Liberalism. | Authoritarianism. | Political science—Philosophy.

Classification: LCC JC574 .G835 2022 | DDC 320.51092—dc23

LC record available at https://lccn.loc.gov/2021034389

Aber schon der nächste Tag brachte eine arge Enttäuschung.
Törleß hatte sich nämlich gleich am Morgen die Reclamaus-
gabe jenes Bandes gekauft, den er bei seinem Professor
gesehen hatte und benützte die erste Pause um mit dem
Lesen zu beginnen. Aber vor lauter Klammern und Fußnoten
verstand er kein Wort und wenn er gewissenhaft mit den
Augen den Sätzen folgte, war ihm als drehe eine alte
knöcherne Hand ihm das Gehirn in Schraubenwindungen
aus dem Kopfe.

The next day brought a terrible disappointment. On the
very next morning Törleß had bought the Reclam edition
of the volume he had seen in the professor's room and he
used the first break in lessons to start reading. But there
were so many parentheses and footnotes that he did not
understand a word, and if he tried conscientiously to
follow the sentences with his eyes, he had the feeling that
an aged, bony hand was slowly extracting his brain from
his skull, winching it out as if winding it around a screw.

—Robert Musil, *Die Verwirrungen des Zöglings Törleß*

contents

preface

Sous quelque angle qu'on le prenne, le présent est sans issue. Ce n'est pas la moindre de ses vertus.

No matter how one looks at it, the present has no future. That is by no means the least of its virtues.

—*L'insurrection qui vient* (2007)

THE ANGLO-SAXON political, social, and economic model, the combination of a capitalist economic system with a liberal form of parliamentary democracy, seemed to work well for Great Britain and its English-speaking former colonies from the end of the eighteenth until the end of the twentieth century—and especially well for the elites of those countries. In the second half of the twentieth century it even seemed to be establishing itself as the major benchmark for all modern societies. However, it has now been visibly unraveling for the past decade or so. The increase in the speed of this decline in the last five years, during the period of the ascendancy of Donald Trump in the United States and the campaign in the United Kingdom to leave the European Union, has been staggering.

There was always a certain tension in the way the Anglo-Saxon model was perceived in Britain and the United States. On the one hand, it was presented as a universal paradigm to which all people in all societies aspired, and the adoption of which would be in their own manifest self-interest. A rule-governed international system of parliamentary capitalist societies was "the solution to the riddle of history which knows itself to be that solution," to use a phrase that Marx uses for a rather different political project (communism).[1] On the other hand, it was very clearly understood (although perhaps never clearly stated) that if the whole world adopted capitalist liberal democracy, the result would inevitably be that "we"—Britain and the United States as political entities, and the members of the dominant socioeconomic groups within each of these two societies—would remain reliably on top. One can see the tremendous ideological power of a construct that combined universalist pretensions with hard-headed self-interest, especially when it seemed to be confirmed by tangible economic and military success. It is difficult, I think, for anyone who grew up in one of these two societies to appreciate how odd it was to assume that these two aspects—the universalist and the exceptionalist—would reliably continue to be correlated forever. Even those who were clearly socially, economically, or politically downtrodden and who might have been expected to have no special motive to accept the ideology did not necessarily find it easy to articulate their dissatisfaction because they lacked appropriate concepts and an appropriate framework. Members of marginal groups with their own theoretical traditions, even if these were deeply premodern, might have had a better chance of seeing the conflict between these two aspects clearly. As the economic and political situation became more troubled for the United States and for Britain, the tension between these two conceptions became harder to ignore and manage. In his own crude way, Donald Trump saw this and drew a coherent, if repellent, conclusion.

The economic crisis of 2008 was directly caused by the deregulation of the banking system, that is, by the application of what certainly look very much like standard liberal principles to the realm of finance. For a while, however, people seemed unwilling to recognize the significance of this fact, and, when they did, their reaction was surprisingly muted. The stress created by the economic collapse, however, had a gradual ripple effect which took a while to propagate. Only eventually, almost a decade later, did it cause the political systems in the United States and Britain to seize up. Whatever the exact etiology, Trump and Brexit have significantly dented the international appeal of a form of society that justifies itself by citation of John Locke, Adam Smith, the *Federalist Papers*, and John Stuart Mill. Liberalism is such an important part of the ideological framework of the Anglo-Saxon countries that the real economic and political decline of the United States and the United Kingdom cannot be expected to be without effect on the fate of liberalism.

I wrote this text in January 2021 while under lockdown during the coronavirus pandemic, just after the United Kingdom left the European Union. Although I do not mourn the passing of liberalism, these reflections also stand in this other, slightly different, political context. In a way the whole text is an indirect lamentation of the loss which the departure of the UK from the EU entails. My unbelievably privileged position as a retired professor with various entitlements (for instance, pensions) makes me relatively immune to the catastrophic economic effects of Brexit. The loss of much of what remained of British political power and influence in the world is something which I think might not actually be so bad at all, but the massive cultural loss that is a concomitant of our severing of ties with the European Union is one I think I shall probably never get over.

Thinking about Brexit and what the future holds for us automatically summons up for me memories of the Philadelphia I knew when growing up there in the late 1950s just before I left to go to boarding school, a place trying desperately to live up to an image of itself derived from a distant past, and fully aware that it was failing in that. Philadelphia had been a significant city in the 1790s, but by 1955 everything important was taking place elsewhere, in New York, Washington, DC, or Chicago. What is more, people in Philadelphia, in some vague and inarticulated way, knew that. My boarding school too lived in a highly stylized past, which I shall describe in this book. Brexit, too, is (partly) about a dream of returning to a fantasy past, in which the population of the UK was racially and culturally exceptionally homogeneous, and the society was powerful enough, and isolated enough on its islands, to be able to make decisions without much reference at all to the opinions, interests, and needs of its immediate neighbors or indeed of the rest of the world. The primary topic of this book is liberalism; a secondary one is the logic of living in a bubble of nostalgia.

Readers may find more about the details of Catholic theology, belief, and practices, about obscure religious polemics, and about early Christian history than they expected and more than they can easily tolerate. Inclusion of this discussion might seem peculiar for a number of reasons. After all I am not an expert on any of this material, and my opinions about it are nothing more than reports of what I heard in 1960 from a secondary-school teacher, who was himself no master of any of the relevant fields even as they existed in 1960. The reason for rehashing this now is the general point I am trying to make with this story. I wish to claim that growing up as a member of a subgroup with its own very dense and highly theoretically reflected history, and with an account of how that history fitted into the rest of the world as a whole, can give one a cognitive advantage at least when it comes to resisting the allure of certain widespread illusions that are deeply rooted and persistently reinforced by the normal operations of social processes. This can be true *even if* the ideology of the subgroup in question is, in itself, not anything that upon reflection one might care to embrace.

Lenin and Lukács both spoke of the need for an ideology for the proletariat. It was not enough to *be* oppressed or even to know that one was oppressed; one also had to have ways not just of expressing the distress one felt (for instance in songs), but of articulating and refining it theoretically and connecting it with a general view of society, human action, and history. One needed something like what Catholicism provided. So I have expatiated at perhaps greater length than some might feel was absolutely necessary about Catholic details. It seemed appropriate to me for these purposes to give the reader some sense of how substantial, how detailed, how interconnected, historically extended, and historically aware this ideological form was. A further reason is perhaps the surprising, and, to me, dismaying, resurrection of traditional religion in Western societies during the past twenty or thirty years. Given my general Feuerbachian approach to religion, which sees it as arising from unsatisfied human needs, I ought really to have expected this resurgence, after the colossal failures of political action which became evident at the latest by the end of the 1970s, and the obscene growth of human inequality since the 1990s, but in fact I was surprised. I expected people to look for satisfaction in much more privatized and esoteric forms.

The difficulty, of course—and in a way this is probably the defining philosophical difficulty of our time—is that we have become rightly suspicious of all totalizing ideological constructions, such as communism and Catholicism. This means that the real total ideology of our era, the conjunction of democracy, liberalism, and capitalism, actually presents itself as something other than a total ideology; in fact, in some of its more sophisticated forms it presents itself as the anti-ideology par excellence.

It is not hard to see through this specific deception, but even when we have done that we are still confronted with an inherently unstable and uncomfortable situation: We seem, for a variety of reasons, to need something like a total worldview, and yet we have reason to believe that none, at least none of those available to us, will be satisfactory. The intellectual life of a moderately observant and intelligent person in our times has to consist of a series of business trips, expeditions, rambles, and almost aimless wanderings through a landscape that is essentially structured by what seems to be this great paradox: that total worldviews seem both indispensable and untenable. Normally, a business trip follows a well-established route to an intended end point, but an expedition is a journey into the unknown. Both of these, however, are strongly teleologically structured activities; they are directed toward a goal (even if the goal, as in the case of an expedition, is the discovery of something new). A ramble isn't like that at all, but is characterized by more internal spontaneity and is responsive at best to whimsy, and the pleasure of the moment. A truly aimless wandering is even less structured. The text that follows tells the story of one individual path through this landscape. In retrospect, I have imposed on it more shape, unity, and structure, and more of a sense of direction than it seemed to have while I engaged in proceeding along it. It often seemed like aimless wandering in a singularly inhospitable environment.

However, it does seem to me now to be true that it is possible to tell it as a coherent tale of the kind I recount in what follows. This in itself is not insignificant because it might not have been possible to do that without an intolerable amount of arbitrary bending, distortion, addition, and deletion. The exact relevance of my account is something I must leave up to the reader's judgment.

not thinking like a liberal

Introduction

Il n'y a pas d'autre monde. Il y a simplement une autre manière de vivre.

There is no other world, just another way of living.

—Jacques Mesrine, *L'Instinct de mort*

LEADING POLITICIANS of contemporary societies in Western Europe and North America like to characterize the regimes in which they operate as "liberal parliamentary democracies." Obviously this is a problematic self-description in a number of different ways.[1] Many of these societies are actually hereditary monarchies, in which feudal religious structures still play some role. In the United Kingdom, the prime minister has some prerogative powers derived from the queen, and not subject to normal parliamentary control, and, as in Iran, religious leaders have political power: bishops have an automatic seat in the upper chamber of the legislative assembly, the House of Lords. On stricter constructions of the meaning of "democracy," no parliamentary regime can be truly "democratic."[2] We also now see attempts to create explicitly illiberal, but purportedly democratic, regimes, as in contemporary Hungary. Still, on the whole, this general characterization of places like Canada, Greece, Norway, Spain, Mexico, the United States, Italy, and the Czech Republic does not seem completely off the mark, especially in view of the necessarily approximate and flexible nature of any kind of description in politics; it is, after all, a general description intended to apply to many different cases. In politics, it is a highly political matter whether one construes certain central terms more strictly or more expansively, and that means that the underlying concepts must at least in principle lend themselves to this, or not exclude it from the very start. In this book I do not propose to discuss "democracy" or the idea of a "parliamentary" regime, although both of those are topics of great importance. Rather I want to focus on the description "liberal."

Some form of liberalism is, in my view, still the basic framework which structures political, economic, and social thought in the English-speaking world. The text you are about to read is not a sociological analysis of modern polities or a set of philosophical or political arguments against the basic tenets of liberalism (no matter how defined) or a critical discussion of the effects of trying to run a society along these principles in a world like ours. All of these would be eminently worthy enterprises, but they are not mine, and anyone who tries to read this book looking for detachable arguments against liberalism will miss the point and be disappointed. It is rather a kind of ethnographic account, with a strongly autobiographical component, of one particular niche in the ecology of modern societies. Large and complex societies will differ greatly in the number and kind of such relatively independent interstitial positions they permit to develop and persist, but one characteristic that most of these niches have is that they are highly dependent on a particular context and sometimes also on a particular historical configuration. The one I am going to describe was certainly fragile, and at the end of this book I shall say something about how it eventually dissolved when a brief historical conjunction which made it possible ended. Still what I am describing is not a mere theoretical possibility, but something that actually could and did exist in a relatively advanced Western society as recently as the early 1960s. This fact, as I shall try to show, has consequences for how we might think about our political world.

The philosophical habit of focused individual criticism of clearly formulated theses is not useless, but it is of limited value in discussing large-scale, historically persistent movements like Christianity, nationalism, or even Darwinism. There are obviously important differences between religions, political ideologies, and scientific theories, but in some respects—such as, precisely, their ability to bring together large groups of people over more than one generation around constellations of relatively abstract concepts and ideas—it is possible to treat them as similar. Refutation (whether by pointing out internal contradiction, weakness of or error in argumentation, or simple empirical incorrectness) is a perfectly useful category, if one has a sharply defined and fixed target in the form of a specific, fully articulated statement, but one of the features of these large-scale movements is that they are not like that at all; they have clear ideational components, which are in some sense essential to them, but they are also in many ways amorphous, open at the edges, and like living organisms in their ability to change (in various ways) while retaining their identity. This is also not merely a defect or disadvantage; their open texture is part of what makes them valuable. They are not just descriptions of existing reality, but are also programs for future research, theoretical development, and action. The ability to change, adapt, and develop is part of what they essentially are. They are intended, among other things, to guide us through an uncertain future, in particular to help us to make decisions vis-à-vis *new* unknown situations and form new opinions about them. Thus they need to be inherently open to variation, evolution, and change.

To be more exact, there are three things one must keep in mind in thinking about such movements. First, there is the Nietzschean point, which I just mentioned—namely, that they have no definition in the strict sense.[3] They have a history, and at any time in that history their myriad variants share enough properties to allow us to identify them as instances of the same thing (for instance, Christian sects, as opposed to Platonic schools). Certain things are more central to them than others: for instance, belief in the resurrection of the dead is more central to most early forms of Christianity than, say, vegetarianism—which some sects also practiced.[4] However, all this can change, and attitudes or beliefs that seemed central at one point can become peripheral (or even be dropped, such as a prohibition on taking oaths or on working as a money-changer), while others can shift into the center of the movement, as for instance the obsession with certain items of sexual morality which has risen to special prominence in some recent versions of Christianity.

Second, there is a general point about the role of "refutation," which is derived from Thomas Kuhn and the subsequent discussion of his work.[5] Whatever might be true in an ideal world, it is simply *not* true that the way in which science advances through time is by a simple two-step process: at first people hold to, say, Darwinism until one of the apparent individual constituents of the theory is "refuted" (by showing it is incompatible with other constituents or with reality), and then, in a second step, as soon as such a refutation appears, the underlying theoretical approach is abandoned wholesale. Movements are infinitely fertile in discovering ways to obviate or discount apparent refutation, not all of which are inherently reprehensible—because, after all, what seem at one moment to be important objections can eventually turn out to be based on mistakes of one kind or another. Historical configurations like Christianity or nationalism that are not inherently scientific theories can also mutate in the face of opposition or refutation, or, for that matter, just in the face of general historical change. Ptolemy's model of the solar system is perhaps an extreme case of persistence despite a history of failure, where each discrepancy between what the theory would require and actual experience of what was the case was considered merely to be a sign that further fine-tuning of the basic theory was needed. According to Ptolemy, the planets, the moon, the stars, and the sun moved around the earth in fixed circular orbits. On closer inspection, though, the positions occupied by planets, moon, and sun did not seem to correspond to those which the theory would require. Rather than change either of the two central assumptions of Ptolemy—that the sun and planets move around the earth and that celestial motion is always perfectly circular—some astronomers preferred to add to the model further circular motions of celestial bodies around imaginary points to make the result something closer to what was observed. The only reason for the additions of these "epicycles" was to save the theory. The term "epicycle" originally had a clear concrete reference to additional hypothetical movements added to the basic stock recognized by the theory, but has now come to refer to ad hoc additions to a theory introduced into it merely to avoid refutation. There is no specifiable individual point before which it is reasonable to try to save the theory by correction and after which it is not. This makes it much more difficult to distinguish evidence-based assessment from other forces that might be operating to maintain an existing theory. One can in fact and in principle always add such further epicycles, and, with enough time and ingenuity, the day of abandoning the theory because it has been "definitively" refuted can be put off *ad kalendas graecas*.

Third, there is the Marxist point that you won't get rid of religion merely by showing that its claims are false, but only by satisfying the underlying need, the non-satisfaction of which gives rise to it; and one might well think that this point held more generally.[6] Even if, that is, *per impossibile,* you did wean people from Christianity as a specific form of religious observance and belief, as long as people continued to have an underlying need for thinking that their lives were embedded in some kind of external metaphysical and normative structure, all that this would mean would be that you would replace one form of consolation-based religion with another. As long as humans did not find in their social world the security and satisfaction they needed, they would continue to project the satisfaction of those needs onto some other imaginary world, and no amount of refutation of the details of that projection would stop the underlying mechanism from continuing to function and throwing up ever new illusions. Theodor Adorno tried to show this to be true by analyzing the astrology columns in the newspapers of the 1940s. An unsatisfied population that didn't believe in God needed to believe in the stars.[7]

People, after all, do not in general abandon a well-entrenched form of thinking and living that responds to some of their basic needs unless they can see that they have a reasonable alternative to it. A reasonable alternative means one in which the basic need would disappear or be adequately satisfied in some other way. What, though, concretely is a "reasonable" alternative? How do you frame the spectrum of possibilities? What sorts of needs would an alternative to Christianity have to satisfy? What would give those who might be receptive to criticism of some of Christianity's features the assurances they would need in order to be motivated to abandon it? How all-encompassing and plausible would an alternative to Darwinism have to be? Since these are, in a very general sense, political questions, it is not at all surprising that the same kind of issues arise in discussions of political ideologies like liberalism. Liberalism, *as opposed to what*? Furthermore, what conditions would something have to satisfy to be a reasonable alternative to liberalism?

The claim that there *is* no alternative is a powerful and often effective one, as shown by the political career of former British prime minister Margaret Thatcher. In her case, "There is no alternative" really meant "There is no economically and politically acceptable alternative," and what "economically acceptable" in turn meant was: acceptably advantageous to the economic agents with whose interests Thatcher identified. She might actually perfectly sincerely have identified the self-defined welfare of those agents with the national interest; others, to be sure, were skeptical about that identification. However, there is a variant of the "there is no alternative" strategy which has also been highly successful: the generation of false dichotomies. The former British prime minister Tony Blair was the absolute and undisputed master of this form of sophism. If you could get people to believe that the only political choice was to support the US invasion of Iraq *or* to endorse everything the Ba'athist regime in Iraq had ever done, then the task of manufacturing support for the war was significantly facilitated. This is a version of "there is no alternative" because one of the elements of the false dichotomy is specifically formulated in a way that makes it unacceptable.

"Liberalism *or* authoritarianism" is just such a false dichotomy. "Authoritarianism" itself designates a number of rhetorically increasingly extreme descriptions of a purported alternative to liberalism, of which fascism can perhaps be considered to be the end point, the ultimate form of anti-liberalism. To be sure, liberalism is in the intended sense an amorphous and shifting collection of things with a clear ability to renew itself, change its shape, and revise the formulation of its central beliefs. If that is true, then why expect it to have a single opposite? Why should there even be a single sequence of increasingly powerful opposites that all lie along the same dimension? The criticisms of certain of the more characteristic tenets of liberalism are telling and well known, and yet it seems to have survived them, which suggests that its appeal is rooted in the fact that it responds in a particularly satisfactory way to deep human needs and to the vested interests of powerful economic and social groups.

This brings one back to Marx's analysis of religion. Would it be possible to think about political ideologies as similarly rooted in fantasies about the satisfaction of pressing human needs that cannot be accommodated and catered for under the existing social and economic conditions? What would one find if one considered the persistence of liberalism from this point of view? If one takes, as I do, the fantasy of being an entirely sovereign individual as being at the core of liberalism, it would seem obvious that such a fantasy is a reaction to massive anxiety about real loss of agency in the world. This fear is perfectly justified in the world we live in, and so the fantasy is clearly connected to the satisfaction of a real need, even if the form the satisfaction takes is illusory. One difficulty is that actually changing the world in such a way that the fears become groundless would require many people to act in ways that might actually reinforce the view that they are sovereign initiators of action. Also, exit becomes even more difficult to envisage once one realizes that liberalism is not merely *self-imposed* illusion; it does not serve only as an imaginary consolation for frustrated needs, but it actually does effectively and palpably benefit some powerful economic actors. The benefits of liberalism are by no means imaginary for CEOs of the fossil fuel industries, and they thus have both a very strong incentive, and ample resources, to contribute to maintaining it in existence and to strengthening its hold on the population.

So is there, or was there (recently), an alternative to liberalism? Is there one that defies the dichotomy liberal *or* authoritarian, or even the dimension along which this contrast purportedly lies? This book tries to trace the track of one life-path that diverges from the liberal consensus without being authoritarian and to give a thick description of it. It is a possible path, or at any rate it was a possible path in what is now the very recent past, because it is one that some people actually took (me, for instance). The intention, then, is descriptive rather than specifically argumentative. That is, this book is an attempt to paint a picture of a form of life and set of beliefs which is not just possible, but which actually existed, where this is to be contrasted with the construction of arguments in favor of a position or the refutation of objections. Some readers may feel that the text reads more like a work of history or ethnography than like a philosophical treatise, because, after all, they might think, philosophy is really all about arguments, not descriptions, about participating in a dialectic of claim and counterclaim, proposal and objection, and rebuttal and counterproposal. I do not, however share this view about philosophy.

To put it differently, I have always thought that showing that "it is *possible* (realistically) to think *this* way" is a better way of describing the goal of philosophy than the usual—and usually also misguided—attempt to show that "it is *necessary* to think *that* way." I have always been mildly repelled by the idea that philosophy should be understood essentially as a matter of finding arguments and refutations, which is a way of thinking about the subject that should have been put to rest in the fifth century BC after the *Dissoi logoi*.[8] My discomfort with the model of argument/refutation is connected with two other features of the way in which philosophy has come to be done and which I find unfortunate. The first is the gladiatorial structuration of much philosophical discussion. Nietzsche, following Burkhardt, drew attention to the fact that Greek culture was *agon*-centered, and that this was particularly true for philosophy as a cultural practice—although in fairness, since Nietzsche was himself fully capable of reading the relevant texts, he had no real need of instruction from anyone else about this. Does, however, formalized conflict always help to generate understanding and reveal truth? The second feature I dislike is the one which Robert Nozick described in the preface to one of his books. He says he wanted to give an argument so powerful that it would fuse the brain of those who heard and understood it and *force* them to accept it.[9] Even apart from the visibly sadomasochistic element in this, it does not seem to me that an approach that conceptualizes discussion in this way, as the search for this kind of argument or refutation, is the most likely way to attain any kind of understanding of the world. Perhaps that is the major reason why I feel distant from the prevailing philosophical culture—namely, I am not as keen to win arguments or convince people that they must bend to my will, as I am to get some kind of understanding of some basic features of the world. If understanding is a conceptual key, this has consequences for how one can also conceive discussion, not to mention the possibility of collaborative effort.

In view of the fact that this is the general position I hold, I make no apology for the presence of a strong autobiographical component in this text, which in fact is structured around a sequence of events in my life. To anyone who thinks that philosophy should be a pure argumentative discipline from which all autobiographical elements are banned, I would first reply by suggesting that this is impossible, and therefore there is some advantage in being explicit about it: pretending it does not exist will not make it go away but rather just foster hypocrisy and self-delusions of various kinds. Second, why the obsession with purity? My most important teacher of philosophy at university, Sidney Morgenbesser, used to say that behaviorism was the thesis that anthropomorphism was inappropriate in the study of human behavior. I have always thought that this was one of Sidney's best jokes, both very funny and also profound. In a similar vein, but without the humor, I might ask where autobiography would be appropriately located, if indeed it had no place at all in thinking about the sovereign human subject and its vicissitudes.

Since, then, the autobiographical element is embedded in what is basically an ethnological report, I should perhaps reinforce an important point. Many of the positions which I describe—especially, for instance, when I am talking about the content of my religion classes in school—do *not* represent views that I myself am endorsing. They are basically reports about what I was told, so large sections of this are in *oratio obliqua*. I tried to punctuate the account with comments such as "Krigler said" or "as we were told," but this became stylistically irritating, and so I was not always absolutely assiduous in keeping it up. Of course, my memory may well be faulty, though I am actually surprised now to see how much of the material I learned in school is actually still, when I now search for it, in my memory. The instruction I received then obviously made a deep impression on me, although not in every respect in a direction of which my teachers would have approved. However, that is not to say that my recollection is perfect. I cannot guarantee that no later embellishment or further reflection has influenced what I recall. I do try to mark cases in which I know that I am reflecting from this moment more than fifty years later and commenting on, adding something to, or modifying something specific that I recall my teachers to have said.

CHAPTER 1

My Fate

Comment s'étaient-ils rencontrés? Par hasard, comme tout le monde. Comment s'appelaient-ils? Que vous importe? D'où venaient-ils? Du lieu le plus proche. Où allaient-ils? Est-ce que l'on sait où l'on va? Que disaient-ils? Le maître ne disait rien et Jacques disait que son capitaine disait que tout ce qui nous arrive de bien et de mal ici-bas était écrit là-haut.

How had they met? By chance, like everyone else. What were their names? What does that concern you? Where were they coming from? From the closest town. Where were they going? Do people know where they are going, any of them? What did they say? The Master said nothing, and Jacques said that his captain used to say that whatever, good or bad, happened down here, was written up there.

—Diderot, *Jacques le fataliste*

I HAVE SOMETIMES been tempted to think that I was doomed or predestined never to be able to get on even moderately good terms with liberalism, but of course that is complete nonsense. *Moira/fatum/destiny* are archaic conceptions, and while family pressures and expectations might for a while in the early modern period have exerted something like a shadow of full proper "destiny"—"The men in our family have always joined the military and you must, too"—at a certain point the merely sociological nature of such pressures became too obvious to be overlooked, and with the growth of the ideology of individual career choice even this shadow lost its ability to inspire an appropriate sense of utter inevitability, and gradually disappeared. Equally I could never really take seriously the Christian transformation of *fatum* into Divine Providence and the corresponding shift in values, which had as one of its results that instead of garnering high praise for the acceptance of one's ineluctable fate (*amor fati*), individuals were encouraged to heed the Christian invocation of hope, *elpis/spes*—the firm confidence that the world made sense and had some inherent meaning, and that God would take care of his own.[1]

What has always seemed to me perfectly self-evident is that both of these approaches are too simple, and incorrect, because they depend on recognizing a nonhuman intentional agency where none exists. Neither fate nor god exists. Any reasonable attitude toward the world we live in would have to be two-pronged. Metaphysically, if one wants to understand our world it is best to approach it through the late-ancient idea that *tuchē*—contingency—rules all. Finally the universe is just a quivering mass of energy propagating itself in contingent ways (although, of course, we see the propagation itself as obeying detectable physical laws), or perhaps the cosmos as a whole is merely an abstract system of formal relations, flickering randomly in and out of existence. The whole thing may instantiate certain patterns, and, if one absolutely wants to, one can call these a "meaning," but there is no intention, no volition, no orientation to value of any kind and no teleology anywhere in sight, except, of course, where humanity has emerged, become active, and imposed a meaning. When that has happened, one has to add to the randomness of the universe a second prong embodied in Napoleon's observation (as reported by Goethe) that ancient tragedy is impossible in the modern world because destiny has been replaced by politics.[2] The destiny encountered by the young military cadet is the *political* decision which his parents and other relatives made to continue to send their sons into the armed forces as previous generations had done.

Politics is a matter of human intention, choice, and volition. Not, of course, *only* of human decision, because there will be a necessity in the concatenation of events that result from any human decision (whether the agent knows this or not). There is in many cases such a thing as the "logic of the situation." Thus, when the United Kingdom decided to leave the European Union, this decision was to put it at a systematic disadvantage in its major market, because even if, as in fact happened, an agreement was reached to continue to trade with the EU without tariffs, the cost of the paperwork involved in crossing what the UK had insisted must be a proper, palpable border was non-negligible. Now, this situation was one that arose not through any action of the goddesses of destiny, but from a series of complex human decisions. Nevertheless, these had as one of their results that a process was set in motion that had a certain directionality. Recently, it has been proposed by some politicians that now that the UK is out of the EU, it is appropriate to reduce consumer and environmental protection regulations, and workers' rights, to permit the growing of genetically modified crops, and further to deregulate hedge funds, because this is what our present situation—outside the EU—requires. This is the only way for us to get back to something like the state of economic prosperity we were in before we left the union. One cannot deny that this line of argument now has something in its favor. After all, as we now might well ask ourselves, why did we put ourselves through the nightmare of years of negotiations about the terms of exit? What was the point? Surely not just in order to make ourselves poorer. So if we follow the dictates of a certain conception of economic rationality, we must try to exploit what relative advantage we *have* acquired (compared with all those we have given up). That advantage lies in implementing the measures proposed above. This, of course, was not something proponents of Brexit trumpeted as a "natural" consequence of leaving the EU before the vote. They had good reason not to draw attention to it because it would have been unlikely to make Brexit more attractive to voters. That many senior figures in the Labour opposition did not see that exiting the EU would have this consequence is simply their mistake. Of course, again, there is no *necessity* that we will reduce workers' rights, but it now for the first time becomes both possible and desirable in a way that it was not before—a path is marked out for it—and so to avoid it requires a continual strenuous act of political will, rather than being something that is simply excluded by the context within which normal politics takes place.

The French poet René Char used the term "*ornière*" (the ruts made in the road by wagon wheels) for something like what I mean here. Thus, toward the beginning of *Feuillets d'Hypnos*, the collection of prose texts which he wrote in 1943–1944 while constantly on the run from the Germans and the supporters of the Vichy regime, he writes, "*Ne t'attarde pas à l'ornière des resultats*" (Don't dawdle in the rut of results).[3] One can leave a deep rut—simply drive one's cart off the road altogether into the forest—but it requires more energy and concentration to do that than to continue along the beaten track.

Thinking about it in this way, I can now rephrase my initial remark about being predestined not to be on good terms with liberalism. It now means that there were some political and human decisions that had the result of laying out a smooth path from which I could, perhaps, have deviated had I had a good enough reason to do so, or had I been either more perverse, or had conditions been different. But deviation would have required either a greater upheaval of the march of the external world from its accustomed track than actually occurred, or a much greater exercise of my will and moral exertion than actually happened. This is still cryptic, so let me put the case concretely. Why did I think I was predestined not to be a liberal? The reason, following my two-pronged model presented above, is that the complete contingency of events in the world was, in my case, overlaid with the result of (a series of) political decisions. I was predestined not to be a liberal by the political events that took place in the autumn and early winter of 1956 in Hungary, and perhaps also, to a lesser extent in Indiana just before World War II.

From the Counter-Reformation to the Hungarian Uprising of 1956

To explain this requires me to tell a historical story, or rather two historical stories. First of all, during the Counter-Reformation in the sixteenth century, the Catholic Church mobilized to protect itself against the new reformed tendencies in Christianity which had recently come into existence in northern Europe and were spreading. These were what we now call Protestantism. The church strove keenly to win back some of the ground it had lost to these movements, in a number of different ways. One of the better-known forms its reaction took was the formation of new religious orders, of which the Jesuits were probably the most effective and are certainly the best known. It has often been pointed out that the founder of the Jesuit order was a former soldier and that some of the forms of organization used re-

semble those of military formations. The effective subordination of
the individual Jesuit to the purposes of the order as a whole and the
strict discipline imposed on all members have been an inspiration to
many later political groups, not least to some on the political left.

There was, however, another religious order that was founded at
about the same time, less well known than the Jesuits, but central to
this particular story. This is the Order of the Pious Schools (*Scholarum
piarum*), and its members are devoted to teaching, and especially to
the education of the poor. The members of the order are called Piarists. The history of the order is complex—it was banned and dissolved
for a time, then re-established, eventually maintaining a particularly
strong presence in the Habsburg lands, Spain and Austria-Hungary.
It also seems fair to mention that over the centuries the original purpose of "free" education of the poor had in practice to be made compatible with the financial requirements of running schools, so the
schools became fee-paying, and then in some places, especially Hungary, they became rather training grounds of the political, cultural,
and social elite, or at any rate of the *Bildungsbürgertum*. Nevertheless
the original commitment was never completely lost sight of, and bur-
saries were always available for those who needed them. There were
lots of Piarist schools in Hungary before the Second World War. In
1947, however, the Communist Party began to exercise control of the
government in Hungary and accelerated, as part of its general project
of secularizing education, a process of taking over the order's schools
and excluding its members from teaching. This would have led very
quickly to the extinction of the order because it would have lost its
raison d'être. The Piarists fought a rearguard action against this, but
the eventual outcome was not in doubt. Some of the priests moved
to one or the other of the order's other schools outside Hungary; the
closest ones were in Vienna and in Krems/Donau (Austria).

In Moscow in February 1956, Nikita Khrushchev gave his famous speech to the Twentieth Congress of the Communist Party, attacking the "cult of personality" which had formed around Stalin. This had the effect, in Hungary, of seeming tacitly to express a willingness to tolerate reforms within the Communist Party, which duly began in the summer (under Imre Nagy); but by the autumn of that year the reforms had reached a point that caused Khrushchev and the other members of the Soviet Politburo to take fright. After complicated political maneuvering, there was effectively a popular rebellion in Hungary and a violent suppression of it by Soviet military forces in late October and early November. During the last stages of the rebellion 200,000 to 300,000 Hungarians left the country. About 30,000 of them ended up in the United States—so many, in fact, that in the final days of 1956 the Piarists founded a boarding school (with a section for day students) on the site of a former hospital for the mentally ill, located on twenty acres of semi-rural land just northwest of Philadelphia. About half of the staff of this school were Hungarian refugees, some of whom had come directly after the failure of the uprising, and some of whom had moved in an earlier period from Hungary to Vienna. Some of them (including my religion teacher Béla Krigler) had been imprisoned by the Communist regime; most of the other members of the staff were priests from the Spanish province of the order. The boys in the boarding school were a similar mix, mostly Hungarian refugees but with a sprinkling of Spanish-speaking boys from Latin America (whose fathers presumably had in their youth been educated by priests from the Spanish province). The fees at the school, although, as I later realized, very modest indeed by the standards of private schools, were beyond what my father and mother, a steelworker and a secretary, respectively, could have afforded, but the school made some arrangements with my parents so that I could attend.

Indiana to Philadelphia

That is the first story. The second story runs as follows: My father grew up in Evansville, Indiana, and as a young man had tried to escape the working class by becoming a Catholic priest, which was one of the few paths to social advancement open to someone in his position who had no entrepreneurial instincts or commercial skills whatever. Evansville was a railway junction on the Ohio River in the extreme southwest corner of the state of Indiana. It was a gritty and deeply unenlightened place, extremely racist and strongly xenophobic. My father remembered that in his youth there had been public demonstrations of the Ku Klux Klan, revival meetings of the "Holy Rollers," a group of wandering Pentecostal Protestants who met in tents and encouraged ecstatic mass dancing (whence their name), and the burning of crosses in front of Catholic churches (considered a church of "foreigners"). My mother, who was white and from the East Coast city of Philadelphia, often told the story of the occasion on which, visibly eight months pregnant with me—which dates it to October/November 1946—she tried to get on a public bus in Evansville. The front section was full of white people, none of whom, she reported indignantly, would get up to give her their seat, so she moved to the back of the bus and sat down in the section reserved for Black people, where there was space. The (white) bus driver immediately stopped the bus and threw her off for violating Jim Crow.

Of my father's seven brothers, most had worked for a living in a rather straightforward sense: one had been a baker, one a lorry driver, one an autoworker, one worked as a cleaner in a pharmaceutical plant but also did some farming, and one had a succession of jobs (including working in a bowling alley and doing something related to the distribution of nonalcoholic drinks). One brother, my Uncle George, succeeded in building up a small business during the Great Depression. It had been widely noticed that two businesses were counter-cyclical—that is, the worse the economic circumstances, the more they flourished. These were the cinema and alcohol, two forms of escape from reality. George discovered that there was a third, which was beauty products, and so he started a business for distributing shampoos, creams, soaps, and such things, and eventually became—by local standards—well off. His political attitudes are sufficiently summed up by saying that in his will he left his estate to the Catholic Church, on condition that none of the money be used for any kind of advanced educational purpose, because he disapproved of higher education on principle.

The final brother, an older sibling whom my father very much admired, became a Catholic priest, which gave him some standing, at least in the family and the local community. My father wished to emulate him, but did not succeed. He had been sent home from the seminary because of academic failure—he simply could not learn Latin, which was a qualification for becoming a priest in those pre–Vatican II days. At least, this was the version of the story he told most frequently.[4] The experience left him with a permanent sense of intellectual inferiority, an even deeper devotion to Catholicism than he had had before—rejection having increased his commitment—and a determination that his children should have the most rigorous education he could manage to provide for them. Instead of becoming a priest, he did an apprenticeship on the railway as a mechanic and then moved to Philadelphia and worked in a steel mill, repairing diesel locomotives and large cranes. When the chance came up for me to apply for admission and support at the Piarist school, he was very much in favor of it.

A large part of my adolescence therefore took place at the inter-section of a domain defined on the one hand by the world of the steel mill, where my father worked for decades and I occasionally worked (mostly during the summer when I needed the money), and a world of exiled Habsburg high culture in my boarding school. I use the term "intersection" metaphorically, because any integration of the two do-mains that took place occurred in my head. The reason for this was that the school existed in a hermetically sealed bubble within a time warp; the city center of Philadelphia was less than 100 kilometers away, but for all the contact the students in the boarding school had with the outside world—no newspapers, radio, or television were available, and there was only one pay telephone in a cloakroom on the ground floor—it might as well have been just outside Debrecen or Szegéd in 1932. Many years later when I read Erwin Goffman's book *Asylums*, in which he describes the structural similarities in organization and operation of prisons, mental hospitals, convents, military camps, boarding schools, and a number of other "total institutions," I immediately recognized the type.[5] Being thus cut off from the outside world and subject to the control—no matter how benevolent—of a groups of adults all with the same mission, that of turning all the boys into good Catholics, constituted a virtually ideal set of conditions for equipping me with certain skills but also instil-ling in me certain attitudes, beliefs, and values.

The relevance of all this to liberalism is that the Hungarians on the staff had lived through the deeply conservative, although perhaps not strictly speaking "fascist," authoritarian dictatorship of Miklós Horthy in the 1920s, 1930s, and 1940s, the German occupation of Hungary in 1944, defeat and occupation by the Soviets, and then a decade of rule by the rigidly Stalinist Communist Party; the boys in the boarding school knew only the last of these regimes. Whatever resistance any of the members of the order may have had to any of these political configurations was subsumed under their identity as Catholics, and eventually Catholic priests. The Spanish-speaking members of the staff had grown up in Franco's Spain. Where exactly in any of this was liberalism to be found? It was not really even on the map in the school.

So when I speak about being predestined not to be a liberal I mean essentially that the kind of education I received in secondary school constructed for me paths of thinking and reacting and attitudes which made it more difficult for me than it seems to be for other people to embrace certain basic liberal views. That I had exactly *this* type of (Catholic) education was in turn the result of the decisions which a large number of people in Hungary made in the second half of 1956 which eventually resulted in the existence of this school, and my father's political decision to try to send me to this—frankly, in the context, literally outlandish—private Catholic boarding school, rather than to one of the public or parochial schools in the neighborhood. I accepted this fate originally because I was very unhappy at home— what did I have to lose?—and also because, having a weak imagination but a naturally contrarian temperament, I was keen to learn Russian—which was the most subversive thing I could imagine at the time (1958)—and the school offered instruction in Russian. I stayed because after the initial culture shock, I found the environment congenial—or, more exactly, much better than things were at home; I had been right about that—and the teaching fully engaging.

So can the education in a school in Pennsylvania in 1959 really have been *that* eccentric? And what exactly is, or was, this "liberalism" which seemed so out of the question for me?

CHAPTER 2

Liberalism

Individuum? Keine Schimpfworte!

Individual? No insults!

—Nestroy, *Frühere Verhältnisse*

IN THE PREVIOUS chapter I mentioned the Nietzschean claim that it is impossible to give formal definitions of large-scale historical movements like Christianity, communism, or liberalism, but rather that they should be seen as historically shifting packages, or clusters of beliefs, values, and attitudes, embedded in an equally shifting set of characteristic practices and institutions. So how would one describe the liberal package? Liberals tend to subscribe to the principle *De gustibus non est disputandum* and to put a high value on noninterference in the affairs of others, and on tolerance of differences in taste and opinion. They tend to construe what should count as the affairs of others very extensively, and to take as many areas as possible (including religious belief) to be mere matters of taste and opinion and hence covered by the requirement of toleration. They are also in principle in favor of trying to cultivate as far as possible certain forms of decision processes based on what they call "free discussion" and free mutual consent. The resulting decisions are to be enforced with a minimum of violence, subject to processes of adjudication by judges who are impartial or even neutral. It does seem to be the case that liberalism characteristically flourishes in the neighborhood of economic arrangements of a certain kind ("free" markets), though there is some disagreement about its real relation to such institutions. People like me believe that the connection is not fortuitous and that liberalism in general does its best to justify such institutions ideologically. Others, however, think that this is a mis-apprehension, based perhaps on a confusion of liberalism and neo-liberalism, and that only the latter is inherently aimed at justifying free markets and expanding their use as much as possible.

Finally, at the very center of all this is the notion of the sovereign individual as envisaged respectively by John Locke, Adam Smith, and J. S. Mill, a nonliberal precursor of which can be found in thinkers like Descartes. A sovereign individual is a person who has a free will and is capable of free consent, who knows his (let's stay with the mas-culine pronoun) own mind, what he thinks, what he wants, and whose assertions about what are in his own best interests are always to be respected, because he is the best final judge of what exactly they are. Provided his action does not directly harm another individual in one of a very small number of legally specified ways, he is to be left alone, and his decision processes themselves are not to be interfered with except through a very limited range of actions such as providing him with information he does not possess and engaging with him in some rather limited kinds of discussion. Such a sovereign individual is imagined as surrounded by a sphere of intimacy, his "private do-main" to which access is by his invitation only.[1] The political frame-work within which a collection of such individuals interacts should be neutral between different opinions and values, and especially tastes.

The ideal society is one based on freely given consent (after discussion) by grown-ups who have the dignity which comes from being autonomous deciders, masters of their own fate.

This seems to me to sum up most of the characteristic views we attribute to liberals in everyday—perhaps very slightly elevated everyday—speech. Although no formal definition of "liberalism" is possible or would be of any special use, one can distinguish three different contexts of application of terms like "liberal" or "liberalism."

"Liberal": Adverbial, Systematic, Doctrinal

First, one might note that many of the older forms of usage of words like "liberal" seem to be essentially adverbial in their intent, even if syntactically nominal or adjectival. "Liberal" refers in the first instance to the way in which a certain human activity is performed, and is potentially very wide in its application. It means generous and relaxed; its opposites would include "stingy" and "strict." Very many human activities, after all, are governed by rules or general principles that allow for some discretion in their actual application: one can apply them either "liberally" or (for instance) "conservatively," "severely," "constrictedly," or "in a stingy way." So the cook in the prison may be supposed to give each person one ladleful of soup, but can be "liberal" or "stingy" in the distribution, by making the ladle absolutely full to overflowing or something less than that. The policeman can be said to be "liberal" in his use of his stick, that is, in cases of doubt he hits more rather than fewer people, and he does not bother too much about counting the individual strokes. Then one can use the term "liberal" just to mean "generally inclined to be tolerant of deviancy" (from whatever norm is considered relevant), so that one could even speak of one of the more "liberal" members of a military junta, meaning not someone who favors immediate unrestricted multiparty elections, but merely someone who is not *particularly* intent (compared with the relevant other members of the junta) on pursuing deviants (from whatever the norms are considered to be) with the greatest possible rigor and severity. So one can use "liberal" as the opposite of doctrinaire, hard-line, or even small-mindedly vindictive. It is worth noting that these uses seem all to be highly relative to a particular specified context. Even a "liberal" member of a junta or of a Stalinist politburo would be unlikely to count as a "liberal" by the standards of an early twenty-first-century Western-style parliamentary democracy.

The very breadth and flexibility in the application of "liberal" in this first sense, which makes it so useful in general English speech, is what makes it less than fully enlightening in understanding or judging politics. If *anyone* can be described as "liberal" in this very indefinite way—the apparatus of a welfare state "liberal" in its provision of services and the prison guard in his or her distribution of baton strokes— it doesn't really provide politically especially relevant discriminations.

Second, there is the use of "liberal" to refer not simply to a particular way in which a person acts either at a certain time or in general, but to a developed set of interconnected habits, attitudes, and beliefs. These would include, for instance, a *systematic* preference for discussion and consensus, a strong disinclination to use force in a wide variety of areas, and various associated habits of tolerance for deviant opinions, tastes, and behavior. The emphasis here, which would distinguish this usage from the merely adverbial and contextual one, would be not on the fact that the liberal in this second sense has conscious opinions, views, or theories of any kind, but on the systematicity and generality of the attitudes, habits, tastes, and beliefs in question. Since speaking and thinking are two things that humans usually do, any human who systematically practices great tolerance and tries not to interfere in the lives of others will in general have reasons for doing this which may be more or less coherent and more or less conscious, but some habits and attitudes can be established that actually stand at some distance from any particular theoretical rationale that I might choose to give them at any moment, and some may be things that I do not need to be consciously aware of at all. A "liberal" would then be a person who is systematically inclined to discussion, is disinclined to use force except when absolutely unavoidable, and accepts the expressed human preferences of others at face value as a basis for their actions; these will probably be reflected in and accompanied by a variety of beliefs and opinions, but they may be constantly shifting and at best fragmentary.

Third, "liberalism" is used not merely to designate one of a number of frequently found systematic complexes of habits, attitudes, dispositions, and opinions, but a specific doctrine of the kind that has been elaborated and presented by theorists over the ages. In what follows I am interested in liberalism as such a potential articulated doctrine. Given the indeterminacy of much of human action and the distance at which it often stands from any particular individual beliefs, especially any theoretical belief, it is by no means surprising that there will be alternative ways of giving what one might call an "ideology of liberalism," just as there are different ways to conceptualize Christianity or nationalism. Such ideologies are characteristically partly (more or less) descriptive of existing practices and concrete beliefs, partly idealizing, partly aspirational, and partly, frankly, completely prescriptive. In some the utopian element is stronger than in others. Familiar liberal doctrines are those (in the English-language literature) associated with John Locke, Adam Smith, J. S. Mill, and John Rawls (and his followers); they differ along several of these various dimensions and are thus by no means in every respect identical.

In view of this variety I will have to operate with an ideal type which focuses on some of the more central properties shared by very many of the more influential specific formulations. Operating in this way is, of course, giving a hostage to fortune because any particular liberal can always claim that his or her favorite patron saint is *really* not correctly represented in the ideal type and thus that my discussion is irrelevant. This is something that one simply has to tolerate, if one wants to get beyond the infinite piecemeal work of discussing only details and attain a broader view.

Of course it is perfectly possible, if one puts one's mind to it, to decorticate "liberalism" and use the term in a very loose way to encompass virtually anything—and the prestige which the term has enjoyed in some places at some times might encourage some people to do that. Given that the basic sense of the term is adverbial, as I have mentioned, there is nothing inherently wrong with this. This, however, is nothing more than a fact about the plasticity of all linguistic usage. One can use "liberalism" as the noun associated with any one of the various sensible usages of the adjective "liberal," so it can refer to some general properties of broadmindedness, open-handed generosity, acceptance of variety, lack of vindictiveness, and perhaps some propensity to prefer gentle and nonviolent measures over forceful, energetic, and violent ones. However, here, as I have just stated, I am interested in "liberalism" as a specific theoretical doctrine, and the reason for this will become clear if one thinks of this question: Could "liberalism" in that very unspecific sense be the object of university courses, make up a part of the explicit program of political parties, and perhaps even play some role in judicial contexts? "Liberalism" as an intellectual doctrine was, I had assumed, always supposed to have more of an identity and more of a bite than that collection of no doubt well-meaning, but rather mealy-mouthed platitudes. "Liberalism" in that vague sense—"Be nice to each other and don't hit him any harder than you absolutely have to"—would not, in other words, satisfy what Sidney Morgenbesser used to call the "*alta baba* criterion of publishability" (namely, "Never try to publish a paper the basic content of which is something your elderly grandmother could equally well have told you").[2]

Catholic Boarding Schools: Stereotypes

It will come as no surprise to readers that "liberal"/"liberalism" was not at all a part of the normal vocabulary used in my school—why would anyone have thought to use that term?—but it is also true that if some of the more standard positions taken by liberals had been formulated in the language that was in use in the school they would not have been praised. There is an existing stereotype associated with the phrase "Catholic boarding school in the United States in the 1950s and 1960s" which is, of course, not completely off the mark—stereotypes would not survive if there was not some grain of plausibility in them—but which does not fit my school, during the time I was there, very well at all. First of all, it is true that the school was deeply Catholic. There was only one non-Catholic boy in the boarding section of the school, a Calvinist—let's call him "Andras" (not his real name)—and special arrangements were made for him to go to a local Reformed church, but otherwise the life of the school was regulated by collective morning and evening prayers, religious ceremonies of various kinds, and lessons in the subject of religion (from which Andras was dispensed).

One strong stereotype to which my secondary education did not conform is the notion that Catholic morality is obsessed with sexual misconduct and depends heavily on threats of dire punishments in an afterlife. This aspect is especially prominent in literary treatments of institutions that were in some ways like my school, such as that so memorably described in Joyce's *Portrait of the Artist as a Young Man*, especially in the blood-and-thunder, fire-and-brimstone preaching of the Jesuit priest during the religious retreat which the hero goes on. Joyce's description of the Jesuit college where Stephen was a pupil seemed to me, perhaps unfairly—but I had only this text to go on—to sum up the Jesuit approach to education: extreme, highly moralized authoritarianism, great readiness to employ corporal punishment, an obsession with sexuality, and relentless dogmatic Thomism. They all seemed to me, certainly unfairly, naturally to go together. There was no corporal punishment at my school. The nuns in my parochial elementary school had been very "liberal" in their use of whatever came to hand (metal-edged rulers, books, wooden pointers, the large erasers used to clean the blackboard) to beat children who displeased them, and so I was familiar with this kind of regime, but punishment in the Piarist school meant being given extra lines of Latin (usually Vergil) to learn by heart, stern talkings-to in the headmaster's office, and then, if that failed, simply being asked to leave, which did happen in a couple of cases while I was at the school. This last was, of course, a luxury which a school that was not part of the public education system could afford to give itself.

As far as sexual misdemeanors were concerned, attitudes were also much more relaxed than they had been at the parochial school. Sexual delicts did not loom very large in religion classes or preaching, and seemed to be considered simply as lapses due to natural human weakness, like having too much to drink or getting angry without sufficient reason—things to be avoided, to be sure, but not obsessed about. They were, thus, very different from really heinous things like taking advantage of the weak—"sins that cried to heaven" (like things that could be assimilated to the biblical "oppression of widows and orphans")—or being intentionally cruel. To be sure, Jesus was against divorce—that seemed pretty clear—but that tended also somehow to be associated with maltreating the weak and dependent, like oppressing the widow: how was a divorced woman expected to survive alone in the ancient world? In addition, the Old Testament had lots of instances of polygamy, and Jesus was notoriously a *copain* of whores and an opponent of rigorous punishment of female adultery, so there was obviously socially and historically determined variation in the form of acceptable marriage and a certain amount of flexibility was to be shown in making judgments in the general area of sexuality.

It was, in fact, the one Protestant boy, Andras, who always came back from his Sunday visits to the local Calvinist church rather a psychological wreck. Years later he told me that he still could not free himself from the thought that he was predestined to burn in hell-fire forever because of his sexual desires. For a while he became an assiduous reader of Kierkegaard, but although I think this calmed him down in the short term, in the long run it did him no good. Poor Andras, he had his own private hell; he later returned to Hungary and drowned himself in the Danube.[3] For the Catholics in the school, however, "hell" as such was never really an issue. Our religion teacher, Father Béla Krigler, had tried to study for a PhD in philosophy in Budapest but was prevented from writing a dissertation by the Communist authorities. In addition to his many other interests, he was a keen student of psychoanalysis who told us that we must learn to ignore the sadomasochist fantasies of the Middle Ages and the early modern period. I am sorry to say that Krigler had no time whatever for Milton—"There are groans and fiery pits on all sides, but who cares?"—and this meant that I didn't actually come to appreciate the amazing linguistic tours de force which are Milton's poems until much later in life. Hell, Krigler said, did exist, but instead of looking to Milton or Dante, and thinking of hell as involving pitchforks, hot

tar, fiery rain, and boils, one should conceive of it as "permanent deprivation of the Beatific Vision"—the vision of God which was the
final goal of all human life and the only thing that could give complete and permanent satisfaction. I think most of us were convinced
that this was a deprivation we could endure.

A further way in which the school did not correspond to the stereotype of the "Catholic boarding school in the United States in the
1950s and 1960s," and which made it rather exceptional, was that the
teachers were all decidedly anti-Thomist in their general philosophical orientation.[4] They had no interest in the ontological structure of
substances or in hylomorphism, and would have no truck whatever
with such characteristically Thomist ideas as "nature," "human nature," or "natural law." They were particularly resistant to appeals to
a purported "natural teleology" and to treating "Nature" as a possible
source of normative or proto-normative concepts. Nature, of course,
was not evil in itself, but one must not personify it. Nature was not
anything like a person who could be construed as issuing injunctions
or prohibitions to us or giving us advice. As far as "human nature"
was concerned, natural human impulses could be things one should
(in some circumstances) satisfy, there was no doubt about that, but it
was characteristic that such impulses could be satisfied in a variety of
culturally distinct different ways, and "Nature" itself generally gave
no direction for that. Sometimes, however, natural impulses should
not be satisfied but had to be resisted or needed to be transformed.
In fact, if one were looking for what was distinctive about human nature, *resistance* to nature in the form of resistance to or transformation of natural impulses was the most distinctive thing about us, and
it was also the source of all higher culture. "The most natural thing
for man," Krigler would say, "is to turn against his own nature and
do something marvelous that is not in any way 'natural.'" The very

idea that one could simply read off moral imperatives from nature it-self or that an understanding of human nature could tell you what you ought morally to do or that this or that was prescribed by natural law was just so much scholastic rubbish.

The Sovereignty of the Individual

Still, what did this have to do with liberalism? The instruction in my school took direct aim at the conception of the sovereign, self-trans-parent individual which was central to all forms of liberalism. First of all, Krigler said, humanly speaking, no individual, not even the most self-reliant, was truly independent and free-standing; each person was multiply dependent on other human beings, in the first instance on their own families and then on society. Metaphysically, no human being was independent of God. It was also simply not true that most people knew themselves and their inner world better than they knew the basic features of external reality, or that they knew themselves better than others knew them—I don't necessarily know what I think or believe, and I certainly don't know for certain what I want. People often acted on beliefs they did not necessarily know they had, and the human soul was a mass, generally a highly disorganized mass, of conflicting, highly obscure, only partially formed, inchoate, and unstable impulses and desires. These were not in themselves at all easy to discern. As if that were not enough, it was also the case that virtually everyone was under strong pressure to hide some im-pulses and desires from others, and anyone who had survived child-hood would have internalized these pressures. Therefore, all humans had a deep impulse to hide even from themselves many desires which in any case were not all that easy to see. Perhaps one could, by var-ious techniques—philosophic, religious, hygienic, pedagogical, or psychoanalytic—come to a slightly better understanding of oneself and one's desires and wants, but this would always be limited and incomplete, and probably would also be highly perspectival. Even in the best of cases such limited self-understanding would be a rare and special achievement, very difficult to acquire (and to maintain). It was, then, certainly a grave mistake to assume that all adults were, by virtue of being competent, rational adults, automatically psychologically self-transparent. It was even a mistake to think that most people were capable of becoming particularly competent and self-transparent with a little simple tutoring. Furthermore, it was a matter of common everyday observation that others sometimes knew what a given person wanted better than he did himself or she did herself. There needn't be any mystery about this; it was rather the proponents of the complete self-transparency of the human mind who were the mystery-mongers. They were the ones who posited in every person the existence of a dimension of the soul completely inaccessible to others, but also immediately and fully transparent to that person. Why assume the existence of any such thing? So if the sovereignty of the individual required agents to know basically what they wanted, it was clearly a deeply flawed conception.

To the extent to which humans are not always in fact the best judges of what they actually want—and we have every reason to believe that this is to a significant extent true—to that extent, too, at least, they are not the best judges of what is in their own interest. I wish the reader to keep this point in mind because it remains, I think, valid and, frankly incontrovertible, even for those who are not willing to take the next step, which is more open to debate.

The next step, namely, is to ask whether it is even conceivable that "the good" might be something other or more than just what I, for instance, actually or "really" want deep down. This need not be taken to mean that what is good has nothing whatever to do with what I happen to want—it may just mean, for instance, that the good is not cognitively accessible through mere introspection and analysis of what any one individual happens to want. Thus, there could be forms of the good which I could only come to see even vaguely if I were living as part of an appropriately constituted group of people held together, for instance, by faith and the sacraments. It was not just collective discussion that was important, but collective action and experience. This, Krigler would say, was why one needed not only the isolated Protestant conscience, his Bible and his God, but also a church. This was why it was sometimes said that *Extra ecclesiam nulla est salus*.[5] From within that situation I might come to want this good, even though as an isolated individual I would never in principle be able to see it, much less to want it. If any such thing were remotely possible, starting from the position of the sovereign individual would be a mistake. To put this in a nonreligious way—which Krigler did not actually do, but which is obvious once one thinks about it—there might be inherently social goods, invisible from the mere point of view of the individual.

There is, then, no natural, immediate, simple, or at all easy path which leads humans from whatever epistemic position they happen to occupy to a position in which they have self-knowledge and know what is good (for themselves or anyone else). Discovering what is good can certainly not be reliably expected from discussion alone—even from unlimited discussion under ideal circumstances. Discussion is not a universal panacea, given that people really are deeply different and can be expected to discover that more clearly the more they discuss serious issues. Contrary to the view sometimes advanced by followers of J. S. Mill, discussion will not necessarily lead to greater understanding—it can sow division and increase animosity. And greater understanding need not lead to greater willingness to cooperate or to greater forgiveness; this will completely depend on the circumstances. *Tout comprendre n'est pas tout pardonner.* There was a religious sense in which God could pardon all sins, but this was a truth that had no direct analogue in this world, where the question was rather whether or not I would forgive you if you did something to harm or offend me, and under what conditions I might be willing to do that. The world was a place in which forgiveness was a human virtue that was not always forthcoming. Sometimes someone had to be transformed through real experience, as opposed to discussion, and only then could one make progress. Discussion with certain evil people might never be sufficient; they might need much more radical forms of re-education or therapy, neither of which would be completely without any discursive element, but both of which were forms of action that went beyond and could not be reduced to simple "free discussion."

Furthermore, Krigler rejected the basic liberal tenet of neutrality. There were certain limited and well-defined kinds of cases in which it was perfectly appropriate to find impartial judges, for instance cases of minor disputes between neighbors who were in other regards more or less equal in power, position, and standing. However, religious issues were not matters of minor importance (certainly not to believers). To say that one should treat religious issues not as matters of transcendental importance, but as basically things on the same level as tastes or as simple choices, was not to take a neutral position on them. It was to say that one should not hold such transcendental beliefs—at any rate not hold them *as* transcendent truths—and thus to exclude them from appropriate consideration. Perhaps that was right, but it was certainly not a neutral assumption that could be unproblematically incorporated into the very framework of the discussion, while still claiming the impartiality of that framework. To suspend their transcendental status and treat them as if they were just simple matters of taste, opinion, or choice would be a kind of contradiction, because to say they had a transcendental status was to say that they could not in this way be suspended. It was to reject them in a substantive way while perhaps claiming incorrectly that one was merely engaging in a procedural, formal, neutral, or value-free activity.

Claims to neutrality were in any case often just excuses for making a choice but being unwilling to accept that that was what one was doing, and so hiding it from scrutiny. Furthermore, no amount of fiddling with the "conditions of neutral discussion and judgment" would suffice to cancel out real differences in power. This was the post-Habsburg question which would never go away in eastern, central, and southern Europe: Why should we be a minority in your (plural) republic when you (plural) could be a minority in our republic? This question retains its pertinence even if both republics are scrupulous in administering their laws impartially, and even if they both have a very extensive set of measures for the special protection of minorities.

Cromwell at the Siege of Ross

Krigler and his colleagues knew nothing at all about British history or literature, and they were fully aware of the deficiencies of their grasp of English. With so many native speakers of the language around in the immediate geographic vicinity of the school, it was, then, eminently sensible—in fact, virtually unavoidable—to hire one of them to teach English, even if he was not a member of the order, and so that was what was done. The choice fell on an Irish American man who very definitely put the accent on the first part of that compound and treated the course in "English literature" as a kind of mini-introduction to Irish nationalism. He walked us through the history of earlier English literature, but in a rather perfunctory way—

never showing anything like the enthusiasm for Shakespeare or Milton that, for instance, László Magyar, one of the Latin teachers, did for his subject. Magyar would stop in the middle of a class on Vergil, read out loud some passage that was under consideration, and invite the class to admire it: "Do you not *see* and *hear* Vergil's beauty?," he would say. Nothing like that emanated from our English teacher for the 1200 years of literature from *Beowulf* to the nineteenth century. Suddenly, however, at the end of the nineteenth century, he was transfigured, because for him (and thus also for us), "twentieth-century English literature" was basically a study of Wilde, Yeats, Synge, and Joyce—almost infinite amounts, it seemed, of Joyce, whom we were encouraged to see as a master of all genres (except drama) and an unsurpassed exemplar of all literary virtues. One of the pre–twentieth century texts we read with this teacher, though, was one from the seventeenth century which fit into his anti-British, anti-Protestant Irish nationalist agenda. It was a message which Oliver Cromwell wrote to the governor of Ross in 1649, during Cromwell's military intervention in Ireland. Cromwell was besieging Ross and discussing with the governor of the place the terms of surrender. He wrote: "As for that which you mention concerning liberty of conscience, I meddle not with any man's conscience. But if by liberty of conscience, you mean a liberty to exercise the Mass, I judge it best to use plain dealing, and to let you know, Where the Parliament of England have power, that will not be allowed of."[6]

No one, of course, would take Oliver Cromwell to be a precursor or a shining representative of toleration or of liberalism in general, and no one expects a philosophical treatise from the general of an army negotiating with the commander of opposing forces in time of war. Still, we were told, the structure of this reasoning revealed a characteristic hypocrisy. "I meddle with no man's conscience" *provided* he has a Protestant conscience, and not one that enjoins on him participation in the celebration of Mass. Structurally, this immediately brought to mind what Krigler had said in a more general way about liberalism, whose devotees affirmed that everything would be so much better if everyone was a liberal and at least *acted* as if the transcendental truths of religion were just matters of personal taste, but who also claimed to be adopting an impartial or even neutral stance.

Reason

Krigler continued: reason and the main concrete form which it took—discussion—was not absolute, completely self-sufficient, and fully self-grounding, but rather it always took place within a concrete historical context and under a set of conditions which gave it its substance and direction and which therefore limited the conclusions it could reach. To think either that one could completely abstract from the actual conditions under which discussion and ratiocination took place, or that one could correct for them and somehow completely nullify their effect, was a very tempting and powerful human illusion, but an illusion nonetheless. Of course, one could and to a limited extent should subject the conditions of discussion themselves to scrutiny, but the idea that one could do that completely and exhaustively was without foundation. There was also no reason to think that knowing that prejudices existed would in itself make them go away or be inconsequential. What you could see, your tastes, the focus and direction of your attention, your sensitivities (to pleasure and pain, those of yourself and of others) were always going in part to be dependent on your specific historical situation and on a number of other factors, such as your age, education, specific life experience, temperament, gender, innumerable facts about your socioeconomic situation, state of health, and so on. Reason and discussion is always, finally, located. Abstraction is never perfect and complete. We would all very much like to be like Baron Münchhausen, able to pull ourselves up from the swamp of human life by our own bootstraps, but wishing will not make it so. Neither, of course, does it mean that if all we want to do is to put our boots on, we should not pull on our own bootstraps. What is more, falling for Münchhausen's delusion will make one more likely to absolutize what turn out to be accidental features of one's situation. By thrashing around, the baron can cause himself to settle more and more deeply in the mud; the more vigorously he thrashes, the deeper he may sink.

There are some historical situations that are genuinely hopeless in that there is no purely rational or discursive way to solve the problems that make them distressing. The only hope is for a change that cannot be anticipated or envisaged by any amount of thought or discussion, limited or unlimited, free or constrained. A repressive social system which was distorting the operations of reason collapses for one or another contingent, historical reason, and in the aftermath one can see how the distortion worked. Or, in the Catholic mode, God intervenes in history in a completely unpredictable way, by sending his son down to earth, and this discursively and rationally unpredictable and actually uncomputable fact changes everything. It is not the fault of pagans that they are never going to live life to the fullest in this world, despite their own efforts and the intelligence, rationality, discourse, with which they are in every way as amply equipped as Catholics. By no amount of discussion and ratiocination among themselves could pagans ever arrive at the truth of Catholicism. According to Catholic teaching, some religious truths were not simply further opinions to be thrown into the hopper for discussion, but had a different and stronger status than that. No sensible individual believes that he or she can free himself or herself completely from prejudices and misconceptions simply by imagining them away, or reflecting, or talking to someone else, so why should one expect that a society as a whole, even under ideal conditions, could free itself completely by its own efforts? These are illusions of purity, absolute autonomy, and self-dependence which are themselves ungrounded (and, from a religious point of view, sinful in that they are expressions of human pride). Sometimes after the fact we can see what it was about a previous situation that made it impossible for those in that situation to see their environment clearly, but one cannot conclude *post festum* from this that any kind of ideal of full and free discussion, dependent on no contingent factors at all, is even an internally coherent conception.[7] External events and the real external world matter. It is an absolutely crucial aspect of our lives as human beings that we can abstract from the real facts, imagine them away, correct for them, think about them virtually, but this process can never be complete or have a result that is totally pure.

There was a religiously relevant notion of freedom and of free choice, but that was connected with the exercise of free will in the face of God's grace, and this freedom was distinct from secular choice among most mundane alternatives. Choice among such alternatives was generally pretty irrelevant from a religious point of view. Also "dignity," such as was to be the characteristic of the sovereign subject, was a Roman and not a Christian ideal. The Christian should be devoted to "humility." In fact, the Roman conscious of his dignity was a symbol of human pride and a model of all that a Christian must reject and should eschew.[8] As far as being a grown-up is concerned, it might be something that we had to tolerate, but it was nothing to be terribly pleased about. Many of the traditional stories indicate that Jesus preferred children to adults and proposed them as the models for life, telling his disciples that unless they became like little children they could not enter the kingdom of God.

Finally, not all opinions, values, tastes, or lifestyle choices should be tolerated. This is one of those things which is so obvious it ought not to require mention, and the fact that it would even seem to be worth stating is a sign of how an exaggerated and distorted version of liberalism has come to inform our unreflective thought. Perhaps a sheer unexpressed opinion should be completely free—although if it really is unexpressed, the question is how we know about it and why we are even talking about it—but certainly the *expression* of an opinion is an act. And although there are good reasons for avoiding pre-censorship in most cases, even the liberal thinks that calling for the assassination of politician X, who is standing there directly in front of an enraged crowd, is not something that should be tolerated.

A certain kind of liberalism is the very air one breathes in most English-speaking countries, where a basic familiarity with Locke and J. S. Mill is very widely shared, and where features of what pass as their basic ideas are so deeply embedded in the political and social institutions and the public discourse that it can be difficult for someone who does not have a slightly deviant social position or education to get an appropriate cognitive distance from them, and thus to see some of their deficiencies for what they are. Adorno in *Minima moralia* writes that "*Der Splitter in deinem Auge ist das beste Vergrößerungsglas*" (The piece of grit in your eye is the best magnifying glass).[9] Of course, there is nothing pleasant about having a piece of grit in one's eye— grit itself is not in any way inherently valuable, and not all bits of grit actually contribute to acuity of vision—but a piece of grit would acquire a contextual importance if it did permit someone to see something it would otherwise be difficult to see. My peculiar Catholic education was such a piece of grit.

CHAPTER 3

Authoritarianism

Ni Dieu, ni maître

Neither God nor master

—Louis Auguste Blanqui

SO MY SCHOOL was non-Thomist, anti-liberal, but Catholic—OK. But "Catholic" *must*, one might think, mean "authoritarian." After all, Catholicism must be committed to absolute, transcendental truth as formulated in its own dogmata, and even in the existence of an absolute human authority for matters of faith and morals in the form of the pope. In retrospect, though, I have come to the conclusion that the school was both anti-liberal *and* nonauthoritarian. People who think this is a contradiction should reflect further on their own categories, and I hope to give them even more food for thought in what follows.

Three Senses of Authority

Rather than trying to define authoritarianism, an enterprise even more hopeless than trying to define liberalism, let me cite the formula which is most characteristic of it: "You should (or, ought to) do this, (just) because I say so." It is important to note from the start that this is distinct from another formula with which it is sometimes associated and often confused, "You *must* do this (or else)," which is a formula not of authority but of pure power. The distinction between these two things can be seen most easily if one compares the action of a thug or of kidnappers with that of a policeman in a highly legally regulated society. Kidnappers simply overpower me on the street, tie me up and bundle me off, without necessarily saying a word—they may not even speak my language. They simply force me to do what they want and do not necessarily even make any claim that I ought to do what they want; they don't even claim to have any kind of authority. In contrast, the policeman has both a club and a warrant. If he tells you to break up a demonstration and go home, he may well threaten you with his club, but he also claims to be acting on a warrant and with authority. He does not just force you; he claims that you "ought" to obey. The warrant may be false, the claim baseless, the reality may just be the club, but to discuss "authority" at all is to imagine that there is a difference between simply hitting someone with a club, and claiming someone ought to do as the policeman says. Understanding authority means understanding in exactly what sense "should" or "ought" is being used in the formula "You should (or, ought to) do this, (just) because I say so."[1]

So in what way and to what extent did the Catholicism I encountered during my youth instantiate the formula for authoritarianism? Let me start with my experiences in the local parish where my family attended Mass every Sunday. Another part of the fate prepared for me that I succeeded very effectively in avoiding is summed up in the name of the church, the Church of St. Joseph the Worker. This name is a giveaway. Most of the members of the parish were workers in the local steel mill (and various associated plants), and the dedication to St. Joseph specifically in his function as a carpenter, a man who worked with his hands, was repeatedly cited in sermons. The role we were fated to play in the economy was indicated and sacralized. The sermons also very frequently took the form of a description of what we would now probably call some personal or social issue, which was evoked in lurid terms before the resounding conclusion: "*This is how you should act, because the pope says so.*" This was not the beginning of some kind of interpretative or argumentative process, but rather the citation was itself considered to end discussion definitively. The ideal parishioner, then, was "*laborans et oboediens.*"

The general authoritarian tendency of the Catholic Church in the United States, at any rate in the 1950s, was not, then, simply a myth, and, for that matter, one might even extend this generalization to the church as a whole since the Counter-Reformation; still, this was not the whole story for the version of Catholicism I encountered in my school. First of all, some of my teachers mounted a constant and unremitting theoretical assault on authority as a concept. In the religion class, Krigler discussed the general idea of authority and its role in religion. He explained that in English "authority" was used in three ways. First it was used in cognitive contexts as a term to designate a high degree of epistemic competence in a particular field. "Mark is an authority on diseases of the liver" means that he knows a lot about them and that consequently his judgment is reliable. If Mark does know a lot about the liver, then under most circumstances it would be a good idea, that is, highly advisable, to listen to what he says, if one's concern is the liver. Such knowledge gives Mark no power to coerce you in any way, nor should it reasonably generate in him the expectation that you will necessarily do as he says. It certainly does not in itself impose on you any obligation to do what he recommends.

Equally, I may recognize that Mark has this special epistemic competence, and realize that it would be perfectly rational to do as he says, but feel no inclination to do what he proposes. Finally, he certainly cannot expect to give me orders about what to do about my liver, just on the basis of his expertise.

The second use of the term "authority" was in expressions like "Jane has natural authority." This should be seen in parallel to Max Weber's idea of "charisma." Weber coined this concept in order to describe a form of political organization which the biblical texts describe as being prevalent before the monarchy.[2] There was no king, but the people followed a series of "judges." Such a "judge" was a figure who could get many people to follow his (or in some cases her) lead voluntarily or at any rate pay attention to and take seriously what he (or she) said and proposed, just by the force of some unique qualities of personality or because of a striking constellation of unexpected successes (or a combination of both). "Natural authority" had to be visible and palpable; the person who had it looked like someone whose lead one would want to follow.[3]

The third sense of "authority" is the one which is really in question. It is normative, that is, connected with some kind of "ought."

The Greeks had no difficulty with the first concept of "authority," that which belongs to the expert (*ho empeiros* or *ho episteemoon*). Although Weber used a Greek word, "charisma," for the second concept, namely "natural authority," the Greeks themselves didn't really use that word in that specific sense but had a battery of different ways of describing the phenomenon in question, often in terms derived from their polydemonic and polytheistic religious experience. So one found numerous variants of "He spoke like a god" or "Like Orpheus, he had enchanted them." In general, Krigler said, the Greeks were a population that was very open to being amazed, surprised, thunderstruck, but they were also highly fractious and very disinclined to obey one another (voluntarily or not). The dichotomy that came naturally to them was "be persuaded *or* be forced," and this did not leave much room for such things as natural authority; so if you did find you had to describe it, you reached for metaphors or similes from magic, religious experience, or intoxication.

The third concept of "authority," normative authority, is the one that became historically most important and that is still central to our way of thinking. This is the sense in which, in modern societies, people are supposed to think that they "should" follow duly issued government regulations or they "ought" to do as the policeman says. "Authority" in this sense completely baffled the Greeks. They did not even have a word for it. They knew about power, force, domination, rule—they understood all of these very well, Krigler said—also persuasion, respect, permission, ability, and any number of other related phenomena, but "authority" (*auctoritas*) was a specifically Roman political concept, which was so deeply connected with particular Roman institutions, habits, and ideas that it couldn't be easily extracted from these, and even after the eastern Mediterranean became part of the Roman Empire, the Greeks themselves had trouble with this concept because they had no equivalent. Even later scholars had trouble with the very idea of "*auctoritas.*"[4]

This was what I heard in class in about 1959–1960. It was only almost fifty years later, in about 2008, when I happened to be reading the history book by Dio Cassio, a Greek-speaking Roman senator, that I found the actual passage Krigler probably had in mind.[5] In discussing some events in Roman history, Dio Cassio explicitly writes that there is a word the Romans use in political contexts, "*auctoritas,*" for which there is no Greek equivalent: "*ouk estin hellenitzein*" (it is not possible to Hellenize this, to put this word into Greek). It is worth dwelling on this point. What Dio is saying is not that ancient Greek did not have a word for *auctoritas* in the way in which it lacked a word for "tea," "coconut," or "kangaroo." There is no word for kangaroo because the Greeks never encountered one, but the relevant conceptual space for such a word is there. The idea of having a noun for a particular kind of animal was perfectly available to them, and all they would have had to do was associate the animal with a sound or with some visual marks. In the case of *auctoritas* what is lacking is not the word but a whole set of conceptions associated with the use of this word, which give it its meaning. A parallel formation to *hellenitzein* was *meeditzein*, "to medize," which didn't necessarily mean to *speak* Persian, but to adopt Persian dress, manners, and customs, take the political part of the Persians, think or act like a Persian.[6] Similarly "You can't Hellenize this" means "*auctoritas* expresses something that cannot be incorporated or assimilated into the way a Greek thinks about things." Of course, you can try to change the way the Greeks think about things—expand what they can imagine, say, to re-educate them—and by the time Dio wrote, the Romans had had several centuries to try to do that by forcing them to live with some Roman institutions. No internal restructuring of the way the Greeks thought about things would be necessary to "make kangaroos Greek": show them one and give them a word for it. That makes the Romans' apparent lack of success in imposing some of their conceptions on the Greeks only the more striking. Dio does finally explain at some length what the word means—in the end, not very well, in fact; the best he can do is to point the monoglottal Greek reader in more or less the right direction.[7]

One could, of course, speculate that the reason the Greeks had such difficulty with the third concept of "authority" was that for them the exercise of power was characteristically personal and immediate.

Their idea of the power of the people in a democracy was that the people really did *do* various things; they did not just elect representatives to do things for them. Equally, their experience of knowledge or expertise was highly personal. The locus of it was a particular concrete person, not an encyclopedia, or an anonymous university board of examiners, or a medical association, or some kind of trace on a computer system. This made it hard for them to imagine an abstract structure as locus of authority. This, however, is no more than speculation.

Life without Authority

You can see this general Greek difficulty with the whole idea of "authority" by looking at the specific case of Plato. Plato argued in the *Republic* that philosophers could become experts in the Good.[8] They could come to know all about it, to be, as we might say, "authorities" on the Good in the same way that geometers were authorities on the properties of triangles. He also thought that because they knew the Good, philosophers should rule the city. We might formulate this as "Their epistemic authority ought to give them political authority." However, what Plato actually says is something more like "Unless philosophers rule as kings—and that means that political power and philosophy coincide—there will be no cessation of evils for the cities" (ἐὰν μή. . . . οἱ φιλόσοφοι βασιλεύσωνται . . . καὶ τοῦτο εἰς ταὐτὸν ξυμπέσῃ δύναμίς τε πολιτικὴ καὶ φιλόσοφία. . . . οὐκ ἔστι κακῶν παῦλα. . . . τοῖς πόλεσι, 473D). The beginning of understanding the modern phenomenon of "authority" lies in seeing just how far "our" formulation departs from the Greek one. First of all, "rule as king" (*basileusontai*) is an exceedingly deadpan and disillusioned version of "have political authority." Plato drives the point home by adding that it is political *power* (*dynamis*) and philosophy that must coincide. Second, the modern formulation is clogged with "oughts" in a way that the Greek one is not: "It *ought* to be the case that those who know the Good *ought* to be obeyed."

Lenin once said that a revolution is the most authoritarian thing in the world, but I think that is incorrect.[9] Perhaps revolutions had to be violent, but, as Krigler kept saying, force, coercion, and violence could accompany authority in various complex ways, embellishing it, reinforcing it, elaborating it, facilitating it, and creating conditions within which it might flourish, but that was not at all the same thing. The Greeks had a perfectly good grasp of force and violence (*bia, kratos,* etc.) and its role in human (and divine) affairs, and a clear notion of what a *stasis* (tumult, civil war) was: one party rising up, killing its opponents or driving them into exile, and reordering the city according to its own taste. Thucydides describes the process with some subtlety and in great detail.[10] The Greeks also had a very clear notion of "persuasion" (*peitho*) as an alternative to the use of force, but for them "force/persuasion" (*bia/peitho*) constituted a strict dichotomy.[11] However the whole point of "authority" was that it was to be a third thing, something which could not be identified with or reduced either to the use of force, violence, or coercion or to (rational or irrational) forms of persuasion. In the idealized case, the policeman neither reasons with me until he has convinced me to move, nor does he simply hit me on the head until I do so; he tells me to, perhaps citing his authority. It was this purported third thing that the Greeks found it impossible to conceptualize, so that Dio Cassio thought that despite their acquaintance with and numerous reflections on the use of force (in, for instance, the more theoretically inclined historians, such as Thucydides), the power of persuasion (in the rhetorical tradition of Gorgias), and philosophical argumentation (in, for instance, Plato), the Greeks lacked the concept of "authority."

Just imagine, Krigler invited us, a world in which the very idea of normative authority is absent. And this was the Greeks, who did geometry, philosophy, history, and politics very well without it (thank you very much) and in addition, of course, wrote epics, tragedies, epigrams, odes, comedies, dialogues, elegies, satyr plays, idylls, and other things, sculpted statues, painted their pottery, built temples, designed cities, and sailed around the whole of the Mediterranean busying themselves with war, diplomacy, exploration, piracy, settlement, and trade. So one could easily have a very high level of culture without developing (or seeming to need) any concept of "authority." Words could, of course, be extracted from their original context and formalized so that their use could continue even long after the original set of institutions in which they made some sense had disappeared, but in the case of "authority" the extraction had not shown itself to be conceptually especially fortunate, and the concept remained irremediably woolly and prone to generate confusion. So, of course, there was no reason to eschew its use in many contexts in everyday life where it was sufficiently well connected to be perfectly comprehensible and useful, but no theoretical weight should ever be put on it.

CHAPTER 4

Religion, Language, and History

Darumb sol hie zuschmeyssen, wurgen und stechen heym-
lich odder offentlich, wer da kan . . . gleich als wenn man
eynen tollen hund totschlahen mus. . . . Es gillt auch nicht
hie gedult odder barmhertzickeyt. Es ist des schwerds und
zorns zeyt hie und nicht der gnaden zeyt . . . Drumb lieb
herren. . . . / Steche / schlahe / würge hie wer da kan.

Therefore whoever is able should smash them up, strangle
them, stab them secretly or publicly . . . just as one kills a
rabid dog. . . . Here is not the place for patience or mercy.
It is the time for the sword and wrath, not for grace. . . .
Therefore, dear masters, . . . whoever is able, let him stab,
strike, strangle.

—Luther's advice to princes on how to treat the
rebellious peasants (*On the thieving,*
murderous bands of peasants)

KRIGLER'S CRITICAL analysis of "authority" stuck
in my mind (for sixty years now) for two further reasons.[1] First, I connected this account with the idea that religion—which was the ostensible subject matter of instruction—was essentially connected with

real history. It was a complete misconception to think of it as a theory about something formulated in a book. Christianity was not to be found in the New Testament in the way in which the theory of evolution was to be found formulated in the writings of Darwin. Rather it was a constellation of historical events, institutions, and practices with some associated, but shifting, beliefs, and it could not be understood in a way that abstracted from that. Second, the notion of authority came for me to be associated with the idea that religions are rarely easy to read; they are much more characteristically connected with complex and deep-seated hermeneutic issues—that is, with the attempt to make comprehensible what in some sense could not be translated. In particular, as Krigler kept repeating, one couldn't "just read the Bible" without completely immersing oneself in historical linguistics, social and political history, and a vast ocean of theological, philological, and historical commentary. "Just read the Bible" by itself was a truly idiotic injunction.[2]

Translating the Untranslatable Word

To start with the second of these points first, Krigler was constantly telling us that a certain essential concept X "could not be translated": *logos, agape, auctoritas, sarx, pneuma,* etc. etc. The school was unofficially divided into two parts: the boarders, and the day students, who were boys from the immediate surroundings of the school. Although my parents lived in Pennsylvania, their house was sufficiently far away, about a hundred miles, for it to make good sense for me to board at the school, which I did. Most of the other boarders were not very expansive or demanding—after all, they were refugees and some had been marginally traumatized—and even those who tried to maintain a kind of shabby gentility combined it with a sense of noblesse oblige.

The day students, on the contrary, were boys from the surrounding towns, which were increasingly becoming mere suburbs. These students had moved there from the city center as their parents became more prosperous, and were keen to assert and maintain their new status. They struck me as very brash and very entitled. One of the day students once complained, in the aggrieved and peevish voice that they all seemed to affect much of the time, that the exams in the religion class were unfair because all the questions had the form "What is the translation of the untranslatable word X?" Simple logic showed that such questions obviously had no answer, and thus that it was unjust to ask them on exams. Krigler seemed very amused by this. In retrospect, I imagine he couldn't believe that even thirteen-year-old boys could be that naive—after all, by that time we had all been studying both Latin and either Spanish or German for at least a year (and some of us had also started Russian). He first explained that as a matter of fact questions that had no answers were often the most important ones to ask and continue to ask, and then he very patiently and at great length talked about translation, about the inherent difficulties of any process of rendering something written in one language into another idiom, about difference in semantic shading, tone, and register, about the nonoverlapping extensions of words in different languages, and related phenomena. He did not (as far as I can recall) go as far as to make the late-Wittgensteinian (and then Quinean[3]) points about "radical translation beginning at home," but as a native speaker of an agglutinative non-Indo-European language (Hungarian), he did keep stressing that translation was not generally a one-to-one replacement of words in one language with words in another—after all, even what counted as a single word was a matter of convention in many languages. Translation, then, was usually a very complex and circumlocutory process; in fact, translation and explanation couldn't really be strictly separated as two completely distinct things. Despite this, it made a huge, an absolutely enormous difference whether you had a generally accepted single word equivalent in one language for a word in another, or whether you really needed to give a circumlocutory explanation every time the foreign speaker used some word.

So "What is the translation of the untranslatable word?" was a perfectly coherent question to ask—difficult of course, perhaps impossible, to answer, but completely coherent. It meant: "Explain in English, using as much space as you need, the meaning of this (usually Greek or Latin) word for which either there is no *single* accepted English equivalent or of which the usually accepted English equivalent is a particularly gross semantic distortion." The reason, Krigler added, that it made such a difference whether some language did or did not have a single-word equivalent for some concept was that having a single word meant pulling different phenomena together. But pulling different phenomena together was rarely an inconsequential thing to do. The Greeks knew well that the archon or hegemon (or Roman proconsul) had the power to have you beaten, or imprisoned, or worse, and thus that it was a good idea to do what he said, but to add to that the claim that the proconsul had *auctoritas* (or, for that matter, exercised *imperium*) carried with it a connotation that this power was inherently connected with some status the proconsul had, and perhaps even a (conceivably somewhat weaker) connotation that it would not merely be a very good idea to stay out of his way, but that one "ought" to do what he said. This is no trivial *addendum*. Once you had a single word, you could even imagine (falsely) that it designated a single thing which could, perhaps, be transferred from one person or group to another.

I think I now see, in retrospect, that much of this emphasis on the difficulty of translation, on semantic obscurity, and on the universal necessity but inherent pluralism of the interpretative process, was actually directed against what the priests in the school took to be a typically Protestant (by which they meant, I take it, what they thought was the Lutheran) position. Actually, they distinguished two characteristically Protestant positions: (a) *sola scriptura*, that is, the idea that the church should be based exclusively on what could be found in the written texts contained in the Bible, and that such scriptural guidance was guidance enough for humans, and (b) the idea that Scripture could be and ought to be read in a simple and literal way.

Sola Scriptura

Sola scriptura meant that final religious authority was located exclusively in the written texts of the Bible. Krigler would not himself have formulated what Protestants were trying to say in this way because of his reservations about the whole idea of "authority," but—he said—during this discussion, let us adopt, for the sake of argument, their way of speaking.

First of all, what was so special about the written word? Even if the written words in the Bible had standing because they were inspired, did that automatically give them priority over perhaps equally inspired spoken words, for instance the words originally spoken by Old Testament prophets? Wasn't the living prophetic word a better vehicle for revelation than a written text? How did we know that prophecy had died out? Krigler knew nothing about Islam, but if he had, he would have been impressed by the fact that the Qur'an specifically says that Mohammad is the "seal of the prophets" (33.40), meaning, presumably, the last, definitive, one who closes the series. No more will be sent after him. There is, however, not only no such assertion in the Christian New Testament, but Jesus seems to go out of his way to suggest that something like prophecy will continue. All the discussion of the continuing presence of the Holy Ghost points in this direction. There seems even to have been an established niche for "prophets" in many early Christian communities.[4] Did the text of the New Testament have more authority than the inspired thought which the author had when he sat down to write? Did the written word always have to have more authority than a customary practice? Individual humans were fallible, but would the Holy Ghost who was to watch over the community really permit the faithful to develop over generations deeply entrenched false practices? Suppose, however, that one did grant a priority to the written word; this immediately meant that a whole series of issues about texts—their composition, their unity, their integrity, their transmission, and their reception—came to be very pressing.

First, was a text a kind of simple *aide-mémoire* or something more than that? An Athenian dramatist may have noted down the words of his play to help him train his actors—many of whom may well have been illiterate—but this does not mean that he intended the words he jotted down to be absolutely sacrosanct. Of course, there would be flexibility and variation in performance—the author may not have expected anything else. Similarly, a king may lay down the law, and give judges a written memorandum to keep the main points fresh in their mind, but he may issue several different memoranda, and no one of these is at all intended to be "the Law." They are just rough guides. The Law is what he decides, which is a different thing altogether. Eventually, given various changes in the culture of reading and writing, social habits, etc., the actual words themselves—*ipsissima verba*—may come to have independent standing, but that is something that develops gradually under specifiable conditions. Writing things down does seem to have an inherent tendency to make them *seem* definitive, but there is nothing inherent in the practice of writing things down which absolutely mandates that the written words themselves have fetishistic power of the kind that witch doctors and Protestants attribute to them.[5]

Older readers and writers simply did not have the same idea about the integrity of texts which we have and which may even seem self-evident to us. If we look at what have come down to us as "texts" we can often see rather clearly that they are compilations. One very striking example is the book of the prophet Isaiah, which pretty clearly puts together material from very different historical epochs. At a minimum there are three strata, that is, the book of Isaiah has at least three clearly distinct "authors." There is the eighth-century BC prophet, then another (anonymous) writer active in Mesopotamia in the sixth century (usually called "Deutero-Isaiah"), and finally an even later third anonymous writer (called, reasonably enough, "Trito-Isaiah"). We have no real idea how these three bodies of material were put together, but we should not assume that there was any fraudulent intent involved in the composition. It would have been natural, Krigler said, for a follower, or someone who thought he (or she) was a follower or disciple of the great prophet, to add to the written record of his message, bringing it, as it were, up to date. Not only was there nothing inherently wrong with this, but the texts added by anonymous continuators might actually be better than the original. The texts by Deutero-Isaiah were much more interesting than the oracles of the original eighth-century prophet. Just as in Greece, a poet who wrote an "Anacreontic" poem was not plagiarizing Anacreon, and it was not fraud to include that poem in a collection of works by "Anacreon." Anacreon did not, after all, have any kind of monopolistic control over the writing of poems of a certain sort. Some of the poems by (what we would call) imitators of Anacreon were every bit as good as his were. A similar thing was true of histories like the books of Kings, which may have used a variety of older documents, integrating them as best the author(s) could. So there would be a possible history of each of the original documents which were used and perhaps reused over the course of time until the version of the text that had come down to us attained any kind of stability.

Texts of different kinds clearly solicited and required different kinds of reading: Anacreon, the book of Isaiah, the writings of Thucydides, and the Code of Hammurabi were not, as far as we could tell, intended to be the same kind of thing at all. In addition, there was no reason for us to restrict ourselves to readings that would have been part of the intention of the original authors—to the extent to which there were any such individual authors and to which any of their intentions were accessible to us. It was perfectly possible to read a section from Deutero-Isaiah as poetry even if that was not the original intent of the author.[6]

What Christians called the "Old Testament" was patently not anything like the work of a single human author. It was not so much a book as a library of texts of different ages and provenances, in different genres and claiming different standings. Some of it was (supposed to be) history (Kings), some prophecy (Hosea), some priestly legislation (Leviticus), some lyric poetry (Psalms), some general reflections on human life (Ecclesiastes), some of it "wisdom-literature" (Wisdom), and some everyday common-sense advice (Proverbs).

Why think it was right to read *all* of this in the same way, and why try to impose a literal reading on, for instance, the bits of poetry? So the Catholic view was that most of these texts could—and should—be read profitably in any number of different ways at the same time, literally, figuratively, allegorically, and as a presentation of speculative possibilities (eschatologically), and that the literal reading had no priority whatever, and was often singularly inappropriate.

Canon Formation

Sola scriptura required one to have robust views about the integrity of individual texts, but Protestant ideas about the authority of Scripture required a further idea, which was that the Bible formed a closed canon of uniquely sacred texts. Judeo-Christian religious monotheism could not always assert itself against the forces of syncretism, assimilation, and synthesis, but from the beginning its basic impulse was negative and exclusionary: it was a way of *rejecting* "other gods" in the most forceful way possible—think of the prophet Elijah in 1 Kings 19 and his slaughter of the 450 prophets of Baal. The basic tool of the biblical monotheist was not the trowel to build a pantheon, but the hammer to smash idols. Parallel to this, it was essential to the collection of writing which became the Bible to be a corpus which included some uniquely specified texts, but also *excluded* certain things. How did the mechanism of inclusion and exclusion actually work?

In the case of the series of writings which eventually came to form the Christian New Testament, one had to distinguish several historical processes. First of all, during the period between, say, just after 70 AD and 150 AD, there developed a genre of writing "gospels," and these proliferated. Some of them came to be thought to be more weighty, important, or edifying than others—even sacred. We now know of thirty or forty gospels that were written at the time. Then gradually the idea developed that there should be a "canon" (as it has come to be called) of works that are to be considered part of "Sacred Scripture" to the exclusion of all other works. It is important to see that this idea of a canon is not itself self-evident; one could easily have a very much more relaxed attitude toward writings that circulated, evaluating them on an ad hoc basis, and holding some to be more spiritually edifying and others less, without making a Manichean division between genuine and apocryphal.[7] Third, once one had the idea that there needed to be a canon one had to begin to discuss which particular books, among the hundreds that were circulating—"gospels" and other kinds of writings such as letters—belonged inside and which outside. This was basically negative, a process of exclusion by which some writings were radically demoted, marginalized, or even suppressed. That process took place (mostly) in the fourth century AD. The Council of Nicaea, called by Emperor Constantine and presided over by him and a group of senior bishops, played a very important role in this process of selection and exclusion. It is of the greatest importance that it was by Constantine's authority, backed by the whole political and military force of the Roman Empire, that the council met, and by his authority and that of the bishops that decisions were taken about what was in the canon and what was not. Why exactly does the Roman emperor get a voice in the question of which books are canonical? Also, it should be noted that this was about three hundred years after Jesus's death, so how had the church been constituted and how had it operated during those three centuries without "Scripture"?

Projecting the notion of a closed canon of Scripture from the fourth century back into the past is a highly speculative, anachronistic undertaking. In fact, as we know, the book of Isaiah and the Gospel according to John were accepted as part of the canon, and the book of Jubilees and the Gospel according to Thomas were not. So Krigler was keen that we always distinguish the question at what time the Gospel of, say, Matthew was written from the question at what time it was recognized as canonic, as part of "Scripture" (rather than just as a writing that one might read and cite or not, depending on taste and circumstance), and he insisted that these were two things that needed to be kept distinct.

To say that Scripture alone was sufficient and should be the basis of Christianity implied that you knew what counted as a canonical part of Scripture. If you looked at this historically, it would seem more reasonable to invert Luther's slogan. It wasn't that the church rested on Scripture alone, it was rather the reverse—that what counted as Scripture rested on decisions by the church. Scripture had its status by virtue of being accepted, recognized, and warranted by representatives of ecclesiastical institutions.

Taking *sola scriptura* literally yielded a *reductio*. If you really did simply confront some modern person, say, a citizen of Philadelphia or Ankara or Nairobi in 1960, with a text of what had come to be called the "New Testament," this would and could literally mean nothing to him or her because what we call "the text" was actually nothing but a collection of black marks on a page which were the conventional signs of words in *koiné* Greek. Reading the text alone (*sola*) could never be enough because no one was ever just reading the text; one was reading the marks on the page through the lens of two thousand years of scholarship directed at making the meaning of the Greek terms as clear as possible. Or, more likely, one was reading it as filtered through the complex activities of generations of divines, pastors, ministers, scholars, and committees of bureaucrats who produced a translation into English (or some other vernacular).[8] In a more Heideggerian mode (which Krigler favored), one was reading it through the *dual* lenses of two thousand years of commentary *and* of one's own immediate existential experience which, in its own way, affected what one could understand.[9] To short-circuit that whole complicated, lengthy historical process by shouting "*Das Wort sie sollen lassen stan*" (Luther's "Leave *THE WORD* alone to stand on its own") was not cutting the Gordian knot, as Luther may have thought he was doing; it was depriving the reader of all meaning and all possibility of getting access to a nonarbitrary semantic content. The true content of *sola scriptura* was exactly: principled semantic emptiness. Of course, Luther (and others) did not really intend that. They meant not "Read just the Scripture," but "Read just *my* version *my* way." This implied, though, that a certain hypocrisy was built into the project. Luther did not at all like the way the peasant leader Thomas Müntzer read Scripture and called upon the princes to use the sword to convince him of the error of his ways; they were happy to oblige.[10] We, the pupils in the school, read together (in modernized German editions) Luther's letter on translation and some parts of his tracts encouraging the princes to put to the sword the "thieving, murderous bands of peasants." These were both considered to be important points of reference, and there was some tacit suggestion that the two of them in some unspecified way belonged together.

Luther's letter on translation, Krigler said, was a very serious reflection on this process which, if read carefully, was itself a defense of nonliteral translation, and thus it would be perverse to invoke it to justify a literal interpretation of Scripture. After all, the basic thesis of the letter was formulated in what one could only call a metaphor. The translator should, Luther wrote, "look at the unwashed mouth of the common people" (*dem Volk aufs Maul sehen*), meaning something like "use the most popularly comprehensible form of expression possible." First of all, that was not literally intended to mean visual inspection of the oral cavity, and second, the most popularly comprehensible expressions in any language at any time were themselves thoroughly drenched in metaphor.

In any case, if a truly transcendental God really had anything in particular to say to his finite human creations, how could it conceivably be anything simple or univocal? Why assume that our own deeply human particular language, reflecting one highly specific, limited and parochial set of experiences, would be at all a suitable vehicle for this message? Any truly divine speech would bend, shape, distort, and crack our language out of all recognition and would have to be drenched in what would look to us to be tropes, metaphors, paradoxes, and highly figurative and nonliteral linguistic usage that required complex interpretative processes to extract any meaning whatever. Even from our own human point of view, our world is just not as simple as Lutherans would very much like it to be. The right questions to ask Protestants here, Krigler said, were why they were so afraid of complexity, why they had such a desperate need for simple answers to the problems of human life, and why they imagined that God's intentions would be easy to understand.

Infallibility

Krigler's attack on the idea of "authority" continued as he discussed the historical fact that papal infallibility, understandably a particular Protestant bugbear, was a tremendously recent innovation.

It was a clear mistake to think that the principle *Extra ecclesiam nulla est salus* in itself implied any kind of claim to infallibility. If I said to you that you would not survive in the middle of the ocean unless you were on a ship, this does not mean that the successive captains of the ship always knew what they were doing. It was also the case that "church" in Catholic theological parlance did not usually mean exclusively the social institution centered in Rome, but was an imaginative construct designating in the first instance the "communion of saints," some of whom might be alive (*ecclesia militans*), but some of whom were definitely already dead (*ecclesia triumphans*). Something like this, Krigler said, was what made it so difficult for Communists to leave the party even when they fundamentally disagreed with the leadership of the moment. For them, outside the party there was nothing but chaos, meaninglessness, and insignificance, and better a ship moving in the wrong direction than a leap into the sea.

During the Middle Ages and the early modern period, all Catholics had (more or less) recognized some kind of papal primacy—the pope was clearly *primus inter pares* among Western bishops, and individual popes tried to push this as much as they could in the direction of some kind of qualitative superiority, perhaps something on the model of the *maius imperium* which the Roman emperor had—but there was still quite a step from that to a doctrine of infallibility. In fact, all the Eastern Orthodox churches recognized that the pope had a special place of dignity and honor without in any way thinking that he could either exercise final jurisdiction in matters of ecclesiastical discipline or function as irrefutable guide on theological issues. Traditionally, there had been any number of recognized distinct sources of moral and theological guidance in Catholicism. These included (but were not even necessarily limited to) reason, tradition, *consensus omnium fidelium*, revelation (what Lutherans and Protestant fundamentalists call "Scripture," but which is actually a slightly wider category—although wider in a rather problematic way), the church fathers (the writings contained in Migne's *Patrologia graeca* and *Patrologia latina*), the decisions of ecumenical councils, and the *magisterium* of the popes. There was no clear and fixed hierarchy among these sources. Ideally, perhaps, they were all supposed to converge, but in fact it was clear that this did not happen, and so it was always necessary to give more weight to some than to others.

Some of the popes, to be sure, tried very hard to impose a single pyramidal hierarchy on the church with themselves at the apex, but even at their most megalomaniac, they tended to present themselves as final interpreter and adjudicator of a truth that was already there and available in reason, the fathers, revelation, etc. That is, they did not claim to be the sole and exclusive source of infallible truth. The very plurality of recognized sources of guidance in itself represented a hermeneutic challenge, and that meant that orienting yourself theologically and morally involved learning to deal with a variety of different kinds of claims and negotiating between them. It also implied a constant possibility of change. After all, if God manifested himself in history, then the faith itself should perhaps not be conceived to be completely immobile. Correspondingly, then, perhaps humans needed to learn to live in a continual state of uncertainty. *Sola scriptura* was also an expression of Lutherans' inability to tolerate such uncertainty; Cartesians expressed something similar and made it the very lifeblood of philosophical activity. Later, when at university I read John Dewey and Adorno, I learned to call this general tendency "the quest for certainty" and to associate it with "the authoritarian personality."[11] Krigler did not go this far, but he did keep repeating that the doctrine of papal infallibility had not been promulgated until the nineteenth century, so, given the timespans with which the church worked, that was barely yesterday. I later began to think that this was a case of Catholicism imitating Protestantism, looking for its own single, unquestionable authority. Krigler would never have said exactly this. His tack was rather that the doctrine of infallibility as promulgated in the nineteenth century was hedged round with lots of caveats—one reasonable interpretation of it was that the pope had the final word but could only act after he had consulted the bishops, a bit like the "queen in Parliament" fiction that exists in Britain.

This, of course, might be thought to open the possibility that just as the "queen in Parliament" now effectively means "Parliament," so "the pope in consultation with an ecumenical council" could come to mean "the council." A further limitation was that infallibility was said only to apply to the interpretation of *existing* doctrines on matters of faith and morals, when expressed *ex cathedra*. This meant that the pope's reactions to *new* events or doctrines had no special standing at all. In general, Krigler would frequently cite something that one of the recent popes had said, and then explain that since the pope had said it, it had to be taken seriously as a possibility, but that actually it was more plausible to hold a different view.

It is important not to get confused here by mixing up the original ancient Roman concept of *auctoritas* with more modern conceptions. *Auctoritas* is an abstract noun formed from *auctor* which does not mean, as we might be inclined to think, "author" in our sense of that term, that is, "initiator," the person who begins, starts, or undertakes some project, who, as it were, plants the first seed from which something emerges. Rather *auctor* is derived from *augeo* (αὐξάνω in Greek), which means "increase, extend, intensify." My activity as an *auctor*, then, is always essentially directed at some other activity, in the first instance someone else's action, which is conceived as being already in operation and which I extend or intensify or enhance by, as we would perhaps say, "endorsing" or "confirming" it. If one thinks of the Senate as the ultimate embodiment of *auctoritas* in the Roman Republic, then one will note with special interest that the Senate's main activities are two-fold: first, the Senate could discuss the merits of actions that magistrates envisaged undertaking, *provided that* the said magistrates asked the Senate for its opinion—that is, it could consult about what some other person proposed to initiate, if that other person asked it to; and it could issue an opinion on the proposed measure. Second, the Senate could confirm decisions that various popular assemblies had already made. Mommsen calls the second of these "formally necessary" and the first a mere matter of convenience and expediency.[12] In both of these cases the body with *auctoritas,* the Senate, is not the real initiator, but a body which reacts to a question posed to it with an opinion, not an order.

So the typical Roman configuration is that of a magistrate, M, who decides to do something, X, and claims to do it "with the authority of the Senate," which does not necessarily, or indeed generally, mean that the Senate initiated the discussion of X, and certainly not that the Senate ordered M to do X. The Senate is not in the business of ordering anyone to do anything, but of issuing *senatus consulta*—opinions about various matters. So M claims that he decided to do X, for whatever reason, tacitly presupposing that he has the power (*potestas*) to make this decision. He then requests that the Senate back him up, thus "intensifying" or "enhancing" his decision.

This is very different from the modern idea of the "authoritarianism" of a despot, tyrant, or dictator. The authority of such a dictator is construed as his ability, not to give confirmation to what someone else has the power to initiate and wishes to do, but to initiate *new* projects and get people to do what he orders without (too much) resistance. The contrast becomes especially clear if one looks at a couple of examples. Mussolini decides to drain the Pontine Marshes or Stalin decides on the dekulakization program, and they have the power (as the ancient Romans would say) and the authority (as we moderns we would say [although the Romans would not]) to make their people adopt this policy. Stalin, as it were, is ordering dekulakization "on his own authority." Octavian, the later Emperor Augustus, when a boy of nineteen raised a private army ostensibly to avenge the death of his adoptive father (Julius Caesar). He did this although he held no magistracy and without seeking the approval or advice of the Senate. We moderns might be tempted to say that he acted "on his own authority," but it is notable that Augustus himself in the official record of his life and deeds (*res gestae*) is still enough of a Roman not to phrase things in that way. He describes this extra-legal major initiative of his without using the word *auctoritas:* he says he acted *privato consilio*—as the result of a private deliberation, that is, not one ratified by the Senate.[13]

If, Krigler said, one was not convinced by the general reservations he had brought forward about the very idea of authority, and one still wished to think in these terms, in the case of papal infallibility, it was the original Roman sense of authority that one had to use: the pope's authority was to confirm and intensify doctrines already accepted by the faithful, and in fact this is the way in which papal documents are usually couched. "*Res novae*" ("something new") is not a term of praise in papal discourse. The pope is always keen to emphasize that he is endorsing with his authority some long-standing practice or belief of the faithful. To be sure, one can reject the very idea that the pope has an infallible authority of this kind in matters of faith and morals, and when the doctrine of infallibility was introduced in the nineteenth century, the pope claimed that he was simply codifying an existing practice that had existed and been universally accepted for millennia, but the bishops of some Catholic churches claimed they had not heard of this practice and rejected it. Some of them then broke away and became members of what is now called the "Old Catholic Church"—to be sure, the members of this church would not describe the situation like this, but would assert that they were simply continuing to practice their religion as they had always done, while the mainstream Catholic Church introduced the novel, unheard-of idea that the pope was infallible.

Of course, one can note, even if one does not simply reject the doctrine, that it is highly convenient for the pope and his entourage, easily subject to abuse, or dangerous or inadvisable for some other reason. That may all be perfectly correct, Krigler went on to say, but still the doctrine was conceptually very different from the idea that some individual person sits down in his chair one day and gets an inspired new idea which he promulgates infallibly, and orders people to believe. The authority of the pope was like the *auctoritas* of the Roman Senate—an opinion it would be very rash to fail to consult, but not in general binding. Even if a *senatus consultum* had, in some undefinable sense, more weight than merely a recommendation, it was not strictly an order. In the case of the "infallible" authority in matters of faith and morals, this authority was limited in the ways discussed above to the confirmation of existing practice and belief, and to say it was "infallible" was to say that one could not fundamentally go wrong in following it; but that did not necessarily mean that it was the only way. If one wants to get from point A to point B in the mountains, it is highly useful to have the infallible advice that *this* particular path will reliably lead from A to B, and it might be rash in general not to follow that path, but all that is completely compatible with the existence of other paths that also lead to B. It is also compatible with the decision by some individual to follow another existing path (or even to search for another path that is not marked out).

This will seem very thin beer indeed to non-Catholics in the twenty-first century, as indeed it is, but it is also not exactly an incitement to authoritarianism.

CHAPTER 5

Human Variety

*Das menschliche Wesen ist ebenso leicht der Menschen-
fresserei fähig wie der Kritik der reinen Vernunft.*

Humans are as capable of cannibalism as they are of the
Critique of Pure Reason.

—Robert Musil, *Der Mann ohne Eigenschaften*

IN ADDITION TO mounting general attacks on the
concept of authority, the teachers in my school undermined potential authoritarianism in a number of more subtle and indirect ways,
which were more pervasive, and also less easy to specify, but nonetheless effective for all that. It is not perhaps strictly correct to say
that authoritarianism *must* be associated with the idea that there is
only a fairly narrow set of acceptable human lives. In principle one
can distinguish between my insisting peremptorily that you do as I
say without my giving you any reasons (apart from the fact that I want
it), and my claiming that there are only a handful of acceptable types
of life, but in fact recognition of a great variety of human types and
encouragement to deviate from norms and expectations and to experi-
ment with forms of living does not seem to sit well with the ethos of

authoritarianism. How much variety did the Catholicism preached in my school encompass?

Verlaine and Villon

The headmaster of the school, Father Stephen Senje, also taught mathematics—I had him for differential and integral calculus—but teaching math was only his profession; his real love was French literature. I recall very clearly two of his Sunday sermons, one on Verlaine and the other on Villon. Senje talked about Verlaine's dissolute life, his alcoholism, drug addiction, his abandonment of his wife to pursue Rimbaud, his prison sentence for trying to murder Rimbaud, and then about his repentance, and his regrets for his lost and wasted youth. He mentioned the famous photo of the bald, aging Verlaine, looking particularly decrepit as he sat alone at a marble-topped corner table in a Parisian café, drinking what one must assume was absinthe, with what looks to be an inkwell on the tabletop next to his glass and carafe.

He then talked at great length about Verlaine's collection of poems *Sagesse,* many of which had explicitly religious content.[1] However, he also discussed at length one linguistically and metrically very simple poem which did not explicitly mention God at all: *Le ciel est par dessus le toit.* In this poem Verlaine describes the clear blueness of the sky and the tranquility of unspectacular everyday life, and contrasts them with his growing awareness of aging and his growing sense of remorse at how he has spent his life. The poem ends with lines which we heard Senje repeat again and again in different contexts:

> *Qu'as-tu fait, ô toi que voilà*
> *pleurant sans cesse,*
> *dis, qu'as-tu fait, toi que voilà*
> *de ta jeunesse?*

Verlaine in a café (Lebrecht Music & Arts / Alamy Stock Photo)

What have you done, you there, weeping incessantly, tell me,
what have you done, you there, with your youth?

Perhaps this rather sentimental poem will not be thought to be a
very significant recognition of human variety, since Verlaine's life followed one of the standard patterns of the religious life in which deep
sin is followed eventually by repentance. Still, Senje's unflinching and
actually rather admiring description of Verlaine's life, including
some of the episodes that would be most unpalatable to more traditional forms of Catholic morality, could not completely fail to
leave a mark.

The case with Villon was more complex, partly because of the pau-
city of information which we have about him, and partly because of
the absence of any possibility, on the basis of what we did know, of
subsuming him under the sin/repentance schema. It was documented
that he had been involved in a murder and at least one attempted bur-
glary, and, of course, murder was a bad thing. Thinking about people
in the Middle Ages was, Senje said, always a matter of pools of light
amidst great seas of darkness, and in the case of Villon, he suggested,
it was somehow appropriate that the record just petered out without
permitting us to know what eventually became of him. Senje obviously found this fact particularly haunting. Even in the absence of any
particular religious content in any of his poems, or a recorded repentance of any kind, one had to suspend one's judgment on him, but the
very fact that Senje brought him up and spoke about him and the
power of his poetry in such positive and nonmoralizing terms made an
unforgettable impression on me.

In both of these cases, in Senje's sermon about Verlaine and in
his sermon about Villon, the emphasis was on the inherent complexity
of human life, the difficulty of judgment, the unsurveyability of
choices, and the obscurity of eventual outcomes. These psychologically subtle, tentative, and exploratory discourses were about as far
away as they could possibly be, in both rhetorical tone and actual content, from the sorts of sermons I was used to hearing on Sundays at
the local parish church near the steel mill where my father worked.
The latter were either administrative or strongly admonitory, if not
hectoring, and in both variants very heavy-handed.

Religion: Revelation, Ethics, Aesthetics

It did seem to me even at the time that Villon was getting special
treatment, being given the benefit of a huge doubt, *because* he was a

great poet. I found this remarkable, but those who take a more Kantian approach of a kind that is held by very many modern philosophers would find it not so much remarkable as deeply shocking. Kantians insist on two things. First, that one must strictly separate ethics and aesthetics. The beautiful, the agreeable, the sublime may stand in some vague symbolic relation to the whole sphere of the ethical, but an action does not become morally right by virtue of being, say, beautiful, and your final evaluation of a person must be a moral evaluation and should not in any way depend upon the aesthetic qualities of the life the person leads, or on whether he or she did or did not create great works of art.

The second claim is that religion is, or at any rate should "really" be, just about ethics. To be sure, historical religions will also have some cosmological speculations, maxims of prudence, bits of empirical good advice, cultural demands, and ceremonial nonsense added for rhetorical effect, but it is assumed that these can be easily filtered out, and the quintessence of religion that remains will be a pure morality based on principles of reason alone. Such a pure morality will be one whose sole content is the (categorical) imperative to follow truly universal rules. Kant even goes so far as to say that we judge the actions of Jesus ("the Holy One of the Gospels") as good *because* we independently assess them as being in perfect conformity with the categorical imperative.[2]

This is not a view that is likely to recommend itself to any serious religious believer. Thus, Kierkegaard, an author much read and much cited in my school, completely rejected it, arguing in *Fear and Trembling* that what he called a "teleological suspension of the ethical" was characteristic of the religious sphere.[3] When God asks Abraham to sacrifice Isaac, Abraham shows himself willing to comply, putting aside ("teleologically suspending") all the moral considerations that speak against even envisaging this action. If this sort of event is central to sacred history, then Christianity, whatever else it might be, cannot be construed as essentially a kind of rational morality.

Krigler had a slightly different take on this from Kierkegaard's. He kept saying, "In the revelation the ethical and the religious got confused." I was never able completely to discover what exactly he meant by this, but the general direction of his remark was clear, as were some of its implications. First, he meant to assert that contrary to what (he thought) was the Protestant view, "revelation" could be confused. Protestants were fundamentally wrong about how "inspiration" had to be understood. The authors of the writings that went into the canon were inspired, but inspired humans. Since they were inspired, they could not be fundamentally and completely misguided, but since they were humans, they could get confused and make mistakes, and many of the texts in the Bible just were confused. Second, I think it was clear that Krigler thought that Kierkegaard conceded too much ground to the Kantians by adopting their narrow conception of the "ethical." The "ethical" should encompass a much wider range of praiseworthy dispositions, actions, and forms of behavior than those envisaged by Kant as having true moral value. It certainly was not limited merely to following universal principles. Third, to say that the ethical and the religious "got confused" was not to say that they were, or even could in principle be, sharply distinguished. Perhaps a certain kind of confusion was the ineluctable situation in which humans found themselves.

Certainly one point on which Krigler agreed with Kierkegaard (as against Kant), though, was that "ethics" (even in a sense wider than the Kantian) was not to be the final framework for thinking about human life. The examples to which he kept returning were from the Old Testament. Why was someone like Isaac, in his own right a completely colorless nonentity and apparently significant only because of the role he played as a potential human sacrifice when Abraham was tested, even mentioned by name in the Old Testament? Even more to the point, Isaac's son Jacob was, from a human point of view, simply a con man, and in no way morally admirable. That was the point. They are not religiously significant by virtue of their morally admirable characteristics because, as the authors of the stories go out of their way to point out, they have none. This means that the authors are proposing a different, ultimately nonmoral, schema for looking at them and evaluating them. It might not be fully clear what it is—religious truths are rarely clear, to return to the anti-Protestant point—but part of the point must be that charisma (which Isaac lacked utterly) and morality (which Jacob lacked) are not, even between them, everything. In retrospect, it is easy to see how someone like Georg Lukács, who in his youth was strongly influenced by Kierkegaard and assigned to morality a distinct but subordinate place within a wider scheme ultimately structured by religion, could, when he became an atheist, try to replace religion with politics as the final framework for the evaluation of human life.[4]

There was, however, another aspect of Senje's obsession with Villon which concerned not so much the relation between the ethical and the religious as it did the relation between them and the aesthetic. What Senje was saying here seems to me, in retrospect, to have been an anticipation of the philosophical discussion of "moral luck" that took place in the 1970s following the seminal paper on this topic by Bernard Williams.[5] Gaugin had the good fortune to be a genius. So did Villon. This does in fact affect our judgment of them, which would be very different if either had had the moral bad luck *not* to have been geniuses (and not to have produced work that impresses us as profound). Kantians might say we "ought" not to give them any special dispensation merely because they happened to be geniuses, but Williams's point is precisely to deny the force of this.

Senje would have been disposed, I think, to deny that this is a special dispensation—that is, to deny that these were special cases because in general the "moral ought" does not always and invariably have the last word in evaluating humans and their lives.[6] Senje would not have called this phenomenon "luck," because he was, finally, a theist— perhaps he would have called it "grace," but he tended not to *call* it anything, just to defer to it in his actual evaluations. What Senje and Krigler had in common with Kierkegaard (and also, by the way, with Hegel) and which was taken up later by Williams was an unwillingness to accept the unquestioned absoluteness of the ethical especially if that was understood as any kind of following of rules. Morality was an indispensable part of human social life, but it was not the final framework, and that final framework stood slightly orthogonal to it. If one drops the theistic assumptions it is even possible to imagine that there is no unique final structure for evaluation.

Aude Discrepare

Senje also had a further trait which became almost a verbal tic. In his public allocutions as headmaster he kept repeating the phrase "Dare to be Different" as if it were his own private *ceterum censeo*. I think that as an emigrant he and most of the other priests found the massive cultural conformism of the United States in the late 1950s and early 1960s extremely oppressive, and all the more oppressive for not being at all publicly recognized or acknowledged. I recall very vividly thinking at the time that "Dare to be Different" was pretty cheesy and not at all as considered and differentiated as the sort of thing which Senje usually said to us; it sounded like some kind of advertising slogan. Perhaps he thought this was what he was supposed to sound like in his role of headmaster (rather than in the role of priest, which he exercised in his own admirably reflective and exploratory way at Sunday Mass). The verbal phrasing was obviously taken from Kant, whose *Beantwortung der Frage: Was ist Aufklärung?* we had just been reading.[7] Kant defined enlightenment as the application of the maxim *"sapere aude,"* which he rendered as *"Habe den Mut, Dich Deines eigenen Verstandes zu bedienen"* (Have the courage to make use of your own understanding). The phrase comes originally from Horace.[8] Kant's translation seemed pretty prolix: two Latin words became nine in German, but then we were always being told that Latin was an especially lapidary language, and in any case, as we had frequently been told, the boundaries between translation and explanation were indistinct and porous. Still, even in that context, it seemed highly tendentious to claim that *"sapere"* meant *"sich seines eigenen Verstandes bedienen."* First of all, *"sapere"* means something like "be sensible, be prudent, be wise," which is not at all exactly a reference to the understanding (Kant's *der Verstand*) as a special mental faculty or to the activation of that faculty by a given individual. There is certainly no emphasis in this formula, as there is in Kant's translation, on the need to use one's *own* understanding.

As I much later came to think, it is also ironic that Kant cites this passage because in the original context, Horace is exhorting Lollius, the man to whom this epistle is addressed, to read the poets, especially Homer, for guidance *rather than* philosophers.

> *Troiani belli scriptorem, Maxime Lolli,*
> *dum tu declamas Romae, Praeneste relegi;*
> *qui, quid sit pulchrum, quid turpe, quid utile, quid non,*
> *plenius ac melius Chrysippo et Crantore dicit*

While you were giving speeches in Rome, Maximus Lollius, I was rereading the man who wrote about the Trojan War. He indicates what is beautiful, what base, and what useful in a much fuller and better way than Chrysippus or Crantor do.

So Homer is a better moral guide than a Stoic philosopher. Now, to be sure, Kant would have distinguished the moral guidance given by his categorical imperative from any discussion of the beautiful, the ugly, or the useful, but this was certainly not a distinction that Horace would have made. *Pulcrum, turpe, utile* just about sums things—at any event things in the strictly human world—up for him.

It is particularly pointless for philosophers to give good advice. Thus, Horace goes on, Antenor gave very good advice (*Iliad* 3.347ff.), namely, stop the war by returning Helen and thereby removing the reason for it.

> *Antenor censet belli praecidere causam*
>
> Antenor recommends that they cut off the reason [for the war]

This makes no impression at all on Paris:

> *Quid Paris? Vt saluus regnet uiuatque beatus cogi posse negat*
>
> What about Paris? He says he can't be forced to [act in a way that will in fact allow him to] continue to rule unharmed and to lead a happy life.

Paris won't allow himself to be forced—even by the very convincing arguments of Antenor. Troy is destroyed, partly because Paris refuses to be sensible and happy (*sapere, uiuere beatus*). Horace can write the epistle and has learned to "be wise," he implies, partly, or even to a significant extent, by reading a work of literature by Homer. Well, that is what he says. Actually, one might suspect that his conversion to "being wise" had more to do with fighting on the losing—the Republican—side in the civil war, and then turning his coat and becoming a lackey of the odious Octavian (who later became the emperor Augustus). Perhaps he used his own reason—*bediene Dich deines eignen Verstandes*—when he decided that his bread would be better buttered by the victors at Philippi rather than by the defeated Republicans. And indeed one of Augustus's henchmen, Maecenas, eventually gave him a country estate, his "Sabine farm" (*Satires* 2.6). However that might be, if Homer could seduce Horace, inculcating in him a knowledge of what is beautiful, noble, and useful, perhaps Horace thought that by writing this poem he could play Homer to Lollius, or even to the contemporary reader.

Oddly enough, an analogue of Adorno's "piece of grit in the eye" makes an appearance in this epistle in the immediate context in which Horace issues his famous exhortation:

> nam cur
> quae laedunt oculum, festinas demere, siquid
> est animum, differs curandi tempus in annum?
> Dimidium facti, qui coepit, habet; sapere aude,
> incipe. Vivendi qui recte prorogat horam
> rusticus expectat dum defluat amnis; at ille
> labitur et labetur in omne uolubilis aeuum.

> Why
> do you hurry to take out of your eye anything that irritates it,
> but if something irritates your soul, you put off taking care of
> it until next year?
> He who has begun, is already half finished; dare to be wise,
> begin! He who puts off the time for living correctly
> is waiting stupidly for the stream, to flow by [before trying to
> cross the ford]
> but it has continually flowed and will keep flowing forever.

Horace seems to think it is an urgent, but also an easy matter: just take the piece of grit out of your eye and your sight will be back to normal. Do it now—why wait? Living correctly (*recte vivere*) is also a pressing human concern, and Horace presents it as something as easy as rinsing your eye.

Adorno, on the other hand, thinks that there is no "living correctly" in our society. "*Es gibt kein richtiges Leben im falschen*" (There is no right life in a false life), as he puts it in one of his most frequently cited apothegms.[9] Taking the grit out of one's eye is not straightforward, and without it one does not automatically see the world fully, as it really is, but may suffer a cognitive loss (because the grit functioned as one's magnifying glass). The urgency Horace expresses is real, but he assumes that adopting his maxim of daring to be wise and living correctly is simply up to us. The *hora recte vivendi* (hour for living correctly) is any time we decide to pull ourselves together and begin. What, though, if living correctly required a change in the social conditions under which we live, a change that it was simply not in our power to initiate on our own (much less to bring to completion)?

Perhaps some of my negative reaction to "Dare to be Different" was really just a dislike of the fact that Senje—unusually for him—kept repeating this phrase even in contexts in which it seemed only marginally relevant. In itself, I suppose, it is not really any worse than Adorno's "*Ohne Angst verschieden sein können*" (except, of course, that Adorno wrote this down once and then stopped).[10] Still, whatever one might think of the aesthetics of this, it is hard to see "Dare to be Different" as a formula for repression or a demand for mindless obedience.

Krigler, too, loved the sheer variety of human populations. Once, on the subway in New York, he looked around at the carriage full of the most diverse types of human beings, beamed expansively, and said, "Do you not see New York's *true* riches?" He liked not just the biological diversity of human types, but also the great variety of kinds of human personality and of human modes of life. I recall his discussion of character types. What was important, he said, was that sanctity was *not* a character type. "Godliness" might be a specific character trait that was highly valued by certain Protestants, but this was a deeply un-Catholic view. There was no "saintly" character, in the way that there was a phlegmatic character, an irascible type, or an extroverted personality. There was no possible Holy Will that was *one and the same* in all its possible instantiations. Kant was wrong to think there could be any such thing; that was a category mistake. The communion of saints contained an enormous variety of different kinds of people—peaceable and irascible, serious and frivolous, generous and spontaneous men and women and more prudent ones, hermits and coenobites—St. Mary Magdalen, St. Jerome, St. Francis of Assisi, St. Symphorosa and her Seven Sons (supposedly martyred in the time of Emperor Hadrian; one of my own favorites, probably because of the euphony of the names in English—it is too bad that she and her sons probably never existed), St. Ignatius of Loyola, St. Theresa of Avila, St. Blaise (patron of diseases of the throat), St. Joan of Arc, St. Catherine of Siena, Don Bosco, St. Jude (patron of lost objects and hopeless cases) . . . There was nothing interesting which they all had in common psychologically. I recall the first time I saw the monument to the founders of the Reformation in the Parc des Bastions in Geneva: four elderly, bearded white men (Farel, Calvin, Beza, and Knox) in identical robes, sculpted in a highly debased and coarsened imitation of the style which Rodin uses in *Les Bourgeois de Calais*, peered out of a flat, undecorated stone wall.

Unprompted, the thought immediately sprang into my head: "Protestants, so all the same." That was, of course, nonsense (on several levels at the same time) which I immediately dismissed, but the fact that I even had this archaic reaction was a trace of a view that I had internalized in school.

Reformers, Parc des Bastions, Geneva, Switzerland (Inna Felker/Shutterstock.com)

Finally, Senje always strongly recommended that the boys in our school *not* go to confess to any of the priests who lived in the *Konvikt* ("*cum + viveo*" = common living quarters) and taught at the school, and so arrangements were always made to go to a variety of the parish churches in the neighborhood for that purpose. No reason was given for this, but it seems obvious to me that he thought it very important to avoid the kind of spiritual hothouse atmosphere that could easily arise, to give the boys always a chance to talk to someone outside, and to prevent the priests from having to bear the burden of being both the teachers and the spiritual directors of the same boys. We were always to be able to get a potential alternative opinion.[11]

Attribution of Blame

As should be clear from the description I gave of instruction in my school, notions like sin, grace, repentance, forgiveness, and salvation were a constant presence. Teachers also tried to inculcate a clear sense of the difference between true and false and also between right and wrong. Science (in general) told you the truth about the material universe, although it was not infallible on any individual matter at any time, and despite the fact that it was very complicated to say exactly how it did that. Astrology was false because the constellations of stars and planets at my birth did not determine my fate. Compassion was a good thing, but killing people was (in general) wrong, although there could be extenuating circumstances (self-defense, for instance). No one ever suggested that these distinctions did not exist, although, of course, it was sometimes very hard to see where they lay, and in individual cases good and evil could be almost inextricably intertwined. However, there was a notable, and, in retrospect I would say remarkable, absence of finger-wagging in my school and little mobilization of moral feelings of individual guilt in the service of social conformity. There was very little appeal to what I came to think of as the guilt-ridden individual Protestant conscience.

Most anthropologists are familiar with the distinction which is made between cultures of shame and cultures of guilt. Shame is an emotion connected with external appearances, with visibility and with a real existing human group. To be ashamed is to be afraid to be publicly seen by other members of a given real reference group as having some disfiguring and dishonorable defect, which is not necessarily in any sense my fault. Archetypically, the Earl of Oxford, in the famous story, was "ashamed to show his face" at court when, bowing low in obeisance to Queen Elizabeth I, he inadvertently farted, and so he went into self-imposed exile. Guilt, on the other hand, is supposed to be an internalized emotion connected not with how I look to others, but with something which I have done and for which I should feel personally responsible.

At my school we were familiar with this distinction through reading E. R. Dodds's classic book on Greece, *The Greeks and the Ir-rational*. In this book Dodds contrasted modern guilt-based morali-ties with the ancient Greek popular morality. Popular morality in the ancient world was not based on internal feelings of individual guilt, but on shame, and it was centered around public admiration and hu-miliation, visible signs of success and failure. Greeks thought about their relations to each other in terms of honor, prestige, and standing, and aspired to be able to take appropriate pride in themselves and those with whom they were closely associated. Many years after I had left school, in one of his last, and, in my view his best, books, *Shame and Necessity* (2008), the philosopher Bernard Williams took up this old contrast between shame and guilt, and tried to argue for the need to rehabilitate shame.[12] Moral cultures based on guilt were not, as they were so often assumed to be, inherently superior to shame cultures. His argument appealed at various important places to the account which Nietzsche had given in *Zur Genealogie der Moral* about the ori-gins of guilt from an internalization of my feelings of aggression toward others, which I cannot express because of my fear of the con-sequences.[13] With this appeal to Nietzsche, the two-fold "shame / guilt" schema gives way to a three-part structure: moral cultures can be based on fear, shame, or guilt.

Nietzsche, too, gave an indirect answer to another question that might seem an obvious one to ask about Krigler and Senje. The more one emphasizes the complexity, obscurity, and indeed opacity of human motivation—the less fully transparent I am assumed to be to myself—the more difficult it is to ascribe guilt. This, Nietzsche would claim, is a very important observation and one that *ex negativo* throws great light on the origins of the modern concept of the self, including the purported sovereign self of liberalism. Rather than saying that I know myself and my motives clearly, *therefore* I can be held responsible for what I do, one must, Nietzsche thinks, invert this argument. One of the reasons people are so keen to retain the idea of psychic self-transparency (and, incidentally, also to resist the psychoanalytic concept of the unconscious) is that it is what lets us hold people accountable for their actions in a simple, straightforward way. Since I want to blame you and generate guilt in your soul, I *must* insist that you knew very well what you were doing. Krigler would have been happy to accept the consequence: because we could never really know what we wanted or what motivated us, holding ourselves responsible was a complicated matter, as was assigning the kind of blame that was associated with the generation of guilt. He would, however, have added first that we should not be so keen on assigning blame in this way—especially not to others—and that the Protestant insistence that it *must* be made possible to assign blame in that way (to myself and to others) was just another instance of his eternal refrain—that Protestants seemed to need to make the world simpler than it really was.

Krigler, in addition to his keen interest in psychoanalysis, had also assimilated some of the available anthropological material on the difference between shame cultures and guilt cultures. He was perfectly familiar with the threefold schema of fear, shame, and guilt, and used it repeatedly. We should, he said again and again, try *not* to allow ourselves to be motivated by any one of these three powerful human impulses. They were all completely natural and also extremely strong, but we needed to learn to act in ways that were as independent of them as possible. Obeying God's command because of the fear of punishment was the sign of a low-grade human personality—Krigler would have said a "primitive personality." The same thing was true if one was obeying from motives of shame. However, most interestingly, Krigler also was extremely insistent that one should not do what was right because of feelings of guilt, either guilt about what one had done in the past or potential guilt about what would happen if one did not do the right thing. A sense of individual guilt might in some sense be unavoidable, but it was a bad motive for action.

Fear, shame, and guilt might be unavoidable, even if undesirable, individual feelings, but one could also think of them as constituting a kind of spectrum, with one or the other of them predominating at a given point. To give an instance of what I mean, let me contrast something that happened in my school with an experience I had later, in the 1980s.

In the first example, Father Senje was livid; it is the only time I saw him truly angry. We had as a substitute teacher a novice priest who had great difficulty asserting himself in the class. We boys tormented him mercilessly as only schoolboys—who are, as everyone knows, infinitely creative in this domain—could do. He was presented with a continuous series of tiny acts of opposition, minor irritations and forms of sabotage; all of them, of course, trivial, but cumulatively very trying indeed. Eventually, it simply became too much for him: one day he lost control of himself completely, dropped his book on the floor, and ran out of the classroom. Five minutes later Senje appeared and spoke to us. What he said was that we should all be deeply

ashamed of ourselves for having taken advantage of the weakness of
this man. We were here in our own house, he had come to help us,
he was clearly out of his depth, and we had dishonored our class and
the school by our conduct. I simply note that Senje appealed to all
the classic elements of shame morality: the honor of the group, how
things would look, our pride (or lack of it) in being certain kinds of
people. He never asked the question who—which individual—had
done what exactly, or for what motives. Obviously, I am not suggesting that Senje was proposing to cancel out two thousand years or
so of guilt morality, but the focus was on shame.

My second example comes from much later, from 1982–1983. I had
seen my Calvinist friend Andras eaten up with sexual guilt even after
having become a grown-up, but my next encounter with the exotic
realities of the Protestant conscience occurred when I became friends
with Axel von dem Bussche in Berlin. Axel was the last survivor of
one of the failed plots to assassinate Hitler. He was a dyed-in-the-
wool Protestant aristocrat and a former military man, a much-deco-
rated war hero. However, in the Ukraine he had witnessed what he
was told was a mass execution of "bandits," but since he was no fool,
the scales fell from his eyes and he joined the resistance. Since he was
also tall and blond, he was asked to model and explain the advan-
tages of the new winter Wehrmacht uniforms (designed to be worn
on the Eastern Front) to Hitler and Göring at a military review. Axel
equipped himself with a bomb which he was going to hide in one of
the uniform's largest pockets, and at the right moment he intended
to embrace Hitler and then detonate it, killing himself and Hitler,
and, if all went well, Göring too. So he was going to become a sui-
cide-bomber. However the Allies bombed the facility where the uniforms were stored, and the resulting fire destroyed them, so that the
review was called off before it was to take place. He was posted back

to the front and was almost immediately wounded, losing a leg, and this wound saved his life because he was in hospital when the next assassination attempt on Hitler was made—the bomb in the bunker of the Wolfsschanze—so he did not come under suspicion.

When I met Axel, what struck me most was the particular way in which his moral world was structured around his conscience. Even forty years later, he could not forgive himself, but not so much for having failed to kill Hitler—his failure had not been his fault at all. Rather what continued to obsess him was that he had sworn an oath to the Führer, *and yet* had then plotted to kill him. This was clearly an obsession. The Führer was a monster, and Axel had sworn the oath under exceedingly strange conditions which could easily have been interpreted as (mild) duress, but none of this seemed to matter to him as much as the fact that he had broken an oath he had freely sworn; the guilt for that pursued him to the end of his life.[14] I was flabbergasted by this and really had the sense that I had encountered a man from Mars, but I think I had just met a proper Protestant.[15] Fear and shame played no role in this: in fact Axel was universally feted after the war for what he had tried to do. His view still was, though, that Hitler's crimes were *Hitler's* guilt, but Axel's violation of his oath was his own unending guilt. I still find this way of looking at the world extraordinary.

CHAPTER 6

So, Liberal after All?

Toute leur vie estoit employée non par loix, statuz ou reigles, mais selon leur vouloir et franc arbitre. Se levoient du lict quand bon leur sembloit: beuvoient, mageoient, travailloent, dormoient quand leur desir leur venoit. Nul ne les esveilloit, nul ne les parforceoit ny à boyre, ny à manger, ny à faire chose aultre quelconques. Ainsi l'avoit estably Gargantua. En leur reigle n'estoit que ceste clause. Fay ce que vouldras.

All their life was organized not according to laws, statutes, or rules, but according to their desire and free judgment. They got up from bed when they wished: drank, ate, worked, slept when they had the desire to. No one woke them or forced them to drink or eat or do anything else at all. This was what Gargantua had established. Their rule contained but this clause: *Do what you want.*

—Rabelais, *Gargantua*

ADMITTEDLY, NONE OF this—the discussion of Verlaine's murderous attack on Rimbaud, of whether or not Villon was hanged, of Kierkegaard and Kant—was exactly a call to revolution or an incitement to anarchy, but, as I have already said, it was also not an education which would predispose one to any of the more familiar kinds of authoritarianism.

So, if this was not, in any normal sense, a form of authoritarian training, was it not, then, really just a (perhaps very derivative) form of liberalism? Especially, the claims about the great variety of forms of "saintly" life make this sound a bit like Wilhelm von Humboldt or J. S. Mill, or Isaiah Berlin. Doesn't very vocal advocacy of a kind of pluralism of types of life just mean that the church, or at any rate my teachers, were trying to co-opt forms of liberalism to make Catholicism itself look more plausible? Stealing, as it were, the enemies' clothes?

When Appropriation Is Not Plagiarism

This raises some important general issues about the identity of movements and the different modes of cultural appropriation. To start, no actual historical institution or movement that has been able to maintain itself for centuries will really have been completely immobile and unchanging. There is a clear sense in which Catholicism has been in existence for over two thousand years, so to live and reproduce itself for that long Catholicism must have been able to develop new doctrines from within itself, to absorb new material and new views from outside, and thus to engage in controlled processes of change and metamorphosis. Also, no large-scale historical movement or ideology is as exhaustive, internally connected and unitary, monolithic, closed, and coherent as some of them would like to claim. Very few movements are so cognitively disabling that they render their devotees utterly incapable of any coherent thought or correct observation of the world. Catholicism was the final framework for so many people in so many places for so long that they were bound to have had *some* interesting things to say, which they, of necessity, expressed in the only framework that they had available. This means that even in the huge and tedious corpus which is medieval philosophy, there is lots of material that stands in a very loose relation indeed to the purported theological doctrines that form its macro-structure. It is just a question of liberating it; in fact, one intention of some of the early members of the Frankfurt School was exactly to "redeem" (*erlösen*) the past.[1] Perhaps it is a residual thought derived from religion to think that though some people, attitudes, and movements are completely incorrigible, unteachable, and not to be tolerated, none is exactly irredeemable.

This point is, I think, sufficiently important and sufficiently neglected to bear repeating: The fact that some philosopher has bizarre general views about the existence of a normatively binding human nature does not mean that every single observation or argument which he or she deploys about human motivation must be completely wrong and utterly useless. Medieval moralists were not either inherently stupid or unobservant, so there might well be lots of individual things or connections that they were able to see, arguments that they could make, that did not really depend on the implausible theological framework within which they tried to locate them. In fact, one might ask whether it was not exactly *because* their general view of the world was so peculiar that they were able to see some things especially clearly.[2] Of course it is a delicate task to extract the individual insight or, in fact, the important utopian truth, behind the general ideological construct, and present it in a more appropriate way. That is why "redemption of the past" is so difficult. Obviously a truth "extracted" from its theological context won't be the very same thing it originally was, and this is not an unimportant fact about it, but that is a separate issue.

On the other hand, no worldview has a monopoly on truth, and there is no Office of Patents or Bureau of Copyright for general ideas and attitudes. Many worldviews, however, especially monotheistic religious ones, do claim such a monopoly. Catholics sometimes say that "any truth is from the Holy Ghost." However, suppose I said it was now important to be compassionate to those who have suffered in the recent pandemic. What would we think if a Buddhist then said that I was a Buddhist or had stolen the idea of compassion from Buddhism? It is true that Buddhists have a special place in their worldview for the virtue of compassion, but does this amount to a copyright? Similarly, recognition of a plurality of valuable human psychological types and forms of life is not automatically a sign that the brand "liberalism" (as a philosophical and political doctrine) is being invoked, any more than saying that it is important to love one's neighbor (in some sense of that phrase) is to endorse Christianity.

Concepts of Variable Aperture

Especially in competitive contexts, forms of religious and political thinking tend to use concepts which have what I shall call a "variable aperture." In some contexts, the aperture is opened as wide as possible: If you recognize human suffering as the basic fact of life and compassion as the basic virtue, this is enough to be a Buddhist, and all the rest is inessential; if you think toleration is generally a good thing, you are a liberal. Then at other times in other contexts, the aperture closes, and you need to accept not only that certain forms of toleration are generally good things, but that humans have an absolute right to the ownership of private property, that every individual is always to be taken to be right about his or her own desires and interests, and so on. This variability is different in kind from the different uses of "liberal" I discussed in Chapter 2. There the distinction was between mere adverbial characterizations of ways of acting, (more or less coherent) interconnected sets of attitudes, values, beliefs, and ways of thinking and acting, and finally, explicitly conceptually articulated theoretical views; but the idea of variability of aperture concerns merely scope in the conceptual domain.

There is not only nothing inherently wrong with using concepts of variable aperture, it is in any case to some extent unavoidable, something built into our whole capacity to use language, and to that extent part of what makes speech such a boon. In fact, it is the possibility of varying the aperture that makes human speech potentially productive, and that is something of infinite benefit.

Still, however, if one did wish to play the game of historical precedence, it would have to be noted that the idea of the "communion of saints" is one of the oldest in Christianity. The calendar of saints, and the hagiographic stories associated with them—including the literary genre "Lives of the Saints"—have existed from long, long before liberalism was ever imagined, and even a cursory inspection of this material will show lots of stories and claims that modern readers will not take very seriously—signs, wonders, and miracles—but also just the kind of actually existing great variety of human types and of shapes of human life that Krigler drew our attention to. Of course—and this should be something too obvious to need mention, but perhaps is not—from the fact that there exists a large variety of forms of sanctified earthly existence, it by no means follows that all lives, as they actually are lived, are good, or that all sets of psychological dispositions, character traits, and forms of desire are equally good. Some are perverse, some are evil, some may be perfectly natural but are just bad (perhaps in general, perhaps in particular contexts, for various reasons); even the ones that are not bad may be differentially good. So pluralism in itself doesn't mean anything one way or the other for the acceptance or rejection of liberalism (if liberalism means anything substantial).

In retrospect, I think I see that the view which most of the more articulate teachers in my school held was a kind of existentialist Catholicism with the characteristic existentialist hostility to anything that seemed to make appeal to human nature (including in particular any version of Aristotelianism / Thomism). This had a slightly more Heideggerian tone with Krigler (imposition of Greek ontological categories on early Christian faith), and a rather more Gallic, even Sartrean, inflection with Senje. Krigler and Senje had much more affinity with Georg Lukács or Kierkegaard than they did with Jacques Maritain or Cardinal Mercier. I don't think, though, that any of this would have survived had either of the two of them been put through the mill of the training given to most priests in the United States at the time, which was unremittingly and dogmatically Thomist.

CHAPTER 7

Interlude

Nostalgia, a Trip to the City, Arrival

LE MAÎTRE: *Ne sois ni fade panégyriste, ni censeur amer: dis la chose, comme elle est.*

JACQUES: *Cela n'est pas aisé. N'a-t-on pas son caractère, son intérêt, son goût, ses passions, d'après quoi l'on exagère ou l'on atténue?*

THE MASTER: Don't be a tedious panegyricist or a bitter critic. Relate the matter just as it is.

JACQUES: That is not so easy. Does not everyone have his own character; his interest, his taste, his passions, following which he exaggerates or minimizes?

—Diderot, *Jacques le fataliste*

AH, SCHOOLDAYS. The atmosphere of my school was rather dour, and it operated according to principles that were the exact contrary of those that guided most education in the United States at the time. One priest (although not one of those who taught me directly) used to say, "The worst thing you can do to a boy is to praise him" (because this might lead to the sin of pride). When talking to the teachers, we learned to note the slight pause in their speech which indicated that they couldn't think of anything negative to say. Then we knew we had got something right, after all. The fine layer of melancholy and depression that lay over the school was not really (or at any rate not fully) the result of the fact that it was Catholic, but rather that it was Hungarian. As my dear friend István Hont (whom I didn't, to be sure, meet until 1990) would later say, "The Hungarians are a permanently defeated population; who ever heard of a Hungarian having a good word to say about anything?" In addition to this general cultural trait, some of the boys in the school had very recently come through especially difficult times that had touched them directly. One told the story of watching his brother shot down in the streets of Budapest in 1956; another the story of the bone-chilling cold he had felt as a nine-year-old child walking for miles at night through snowy woods to reach and cross the border to Austria after the failure of the uprising. One of the priests, our teacher of Russian, had been a sergeant in the 3rd Hungarian Army during World War II in 1944—the 2nd Hungarian Army had, of course, been annihilated on one of the flanks at Stalingrad in 1942. During the long retreat from the Ukraine he had developed an appropriately Archilochian attitude toward the military: "I said to my boys at the end then, 'Just run away, because this has no point.'" The classicist A. E. Housman once wrote a parody of a Greek tragedy in which the chorus, hearing a blood-curdling scream emerge from offstage, sings:

I thought I heard a sound within the house
unlike the voice of one who jumps for joy.[1]

The voice of one who jumps for joy was not heard very frequently in the school, either. The closest we came to that was when the Latin teacher pointed out to us that the oracular utterance "*ibis redibis non morieris in bello*" could mean either that you would return safely from the war or that you would not,[2] or told the story about Ovid, who, when being beaten by his father for engaging in the trivial pursuit of writing poems, replied to him with a hexameter, "*Parce, pater, virgis, numquam tibi carmina dicam*" (Spare the rod, Dad, I'll never again recite a poem to you). Later philosophers would call Ovid's performance a "pragmatic contradiction," but although we did not have the term for it, the Latin teacher thought this was worth a chuckle.

In school I had the sense, though, that I had a fleeting glimpse of something that was a faint reflection of a long past reality. It was probably the very last afterimage of the late-Habsburg world described by Stefan Zweig in *Die Welt von Gestern*.[3] As is so often the case with emigrant populations, the country left behind is seen in an exaggeratedly rosy light, and that is no doubt also the case with this afterimage. In contrast (to stay in more or less the same cultural context), the school was nothing like the *Kadettenanstalt* in *Die Verwirrungen des Zöglings Törleß*, because it had a serious, intellectually engaging curriculum and good teaching, and it lacked the authoritarianism, the sadomasochistic violence, and the lurid sexual efflorescence depicted in Musil's novel.[4] Perhaps it was the deep melancholy of the place and its residents which prevented either of these last two from flourishing there.

The Trip to the City

The school had a structural difficulty with its scheduling. Given that it was registered as an educational institution in the Commonwealth of Pennsylvania and that over half of its pupils were local boys from the neighborhood, northwest of Philadelphia, it had to close for the Thanksgiving holiday. On the other hand, virtually all the boys in the boarding section were Hungarian refugees or South Americans who had no idea what Thanksgiving was or at any rate did not celebrate it. The Hungarians in particular found the festival bizarre, and could not understand why anyone would voluntarily eat the dry, stringy, virtually completely tasteless meat of the turkey—"that non-airborne fowl," as one of them used to call it. To be sure, *if* you were absolutely starving in the frozen woods in the middle of winter in the seventeenth century, you would eat whatever you could get. Turkeys were indigenous to North America and so stupid that they were relatively easy to catch, so of course in some cases one would eat them; but that was a matter of dire necessity rather than choice. The only way my friends could understand Thanksgiving was as a kind of penitential ritual: Americans ate turkey to remind them of what it must be like to be starving in the freezing cold of a New England winter, and reduced to eating even this.

What, then, to do with fifty or sixty boys in the boarding school while the proper day school was officially closed? It was too far for many of them to go home (Iowa, Venezuela, Virginia) for only a few days, but they had to be occupied in some way. The solution was to have a school trip to New York City. In late November 1962, then, a couple of the priests loaded the boys into some school minibuses and drove us to the city. When we arrived we were distributed around various places where the school had contacts. I had never been in the city before and so did not have a firm grasp of its geography, but I remember that some of us were housed in a kind of community center downtown in a Spanish-speaking area where some Spanish priests of the order were employed; I clearly recall that the streets were cobblestoned. I went with a couple of others up to Washington Heights in the extreme north of the West Side of Manhattan and stayed in the rather cramped but perfectly adequate flat of a friendly Irish American family, one of whose sons was in training to become a priest. All the boys and priests then assembled in various places and walked around the city just looking at things.

I was especially impressed with the bookshops, which seemed to be everywhere and full of interesting books. I was also most struck with the fact that one could buy proper, *new* books and could have some choice in what one bought. My experience with books had been of two kinds. First, there were cheap paperbacks widely available, but they were mostly trashy novels sold in shops of all sorts. There was the occasional work of merit, but it was just a matter of complete chance whether a particular shop stocked anything interesting or not (and the answer was, "mostly not"). My second mode had basically been one of scavenging in used bookshops in the already rather run-down city centers of Philadelphia and Trenton, where what one found was the luck-of-the-draw of discarded books. Of course, neither of these two places, Philadelphia and Trenton, could compare with the density of what was on offer in Manhattan. Given that my experience had basically been one of the complete precariousness and contingency of book culture, I was amazed, then, by bookshops where one had a reliable choice of interesting, substantial new books. The books were even organized into categories, rather than simply being displayed in random confusion on a rotating wire stand. Unfortunately, I also immediately saw that the prices were, for me, prohibitive. Still, the shops were *there.*

Krigler was keen on modern art in general and the range of things he liked was broad, including notably surrealism and various kinds of nonrepresentational painting. Dalí and the Picasso of the late 1920s and 1930s seemed to be particular favorites. For instance, one afternoon he brought into the Academia Calasanctiana—a discussion group he ran at the school—a reproduction of a work by Picasso from 1930, which depicted a woman on a beach, but the woman seemed to be made at least partly from bits of driftwood.

He expressed his great admiration of the picture and asked us all to comment on it. He took it as a representation of the modern subject. It was as fully self-transparent as anything Descartes could have wished, but it was so by virtue of being utterly empty. You could see right through it. There was not even a place for a proper inner life. This was an image of a psychic wreck, a hollow space partially surrounded by a merely residual structure made of driftwood.

Krigler organized a small group of us to go to the Museum of Modern Art to see *Guernica*, which was at the time still hanging there, displayed by itself in a room on the other walls of which were photos of previous stages in the process through which Picasso put it before settling on the final version. I also wandered into the room in which the triptych version of Monet's *Water Lilies* was exhibited. It, too, had a full room to itself and the triptychs were disposed continuously on a kind of wrap-around partition, so that the viewer had the feeling of being partially surrounded by it. I recall having a similar feeling about both works: "Too much." The Picasso was insisting too much and was simply too big, and the Monet gave me a kind of cloying sensory overload. Visual arts, I decided, were simply not for me.

On this rather downbeat note, we all piled back into the minibuses and drove back to Pennsylvania. I, however, had been sufficiently positively impressed by what I had seen in Manhattan to be very pleased when Krigler told me that, looking at the various universities that seemed to him to be appropriate for me, he thought Columbia would suit me best; so that is where I applied to study. In

Picasso, *Seated Bather* (1930)

(Digital image © The Museum of Modern Art / Licensed by SCALA / Art Resource, NY)

June 1963 I graduated, spent the summer laboring in the steel mill in Pennsylvania where my father worked, to make some money to top up the financial support I got from the university, and arrived in September 1963 on Morningside Heights on the West Side of Manhattan to start my studies at Columbia College. I was sixteen years old, very naive and inexperienced, and still highly impressionable.

Arrival

I was not excessively interested in current affairs before I went to boarding school, but I had vaguely kept up on what was going on in the world, as this was presented to me by the sources of news available (newspapers, radio). I do recall the announcement on the radio of the execution of the Julius and Ethel Rosenberg. It was a Saturday morning, and they had been electrocuted Friday evening, and I remember being surprised because I had somehow got it into my head that people were always executed at dawn. It was only years later that I discovered that the execution had been rushed through to prevent them from making a final appeal against their sentence on the weekend. I followed the progress of McCarthyism as best I could because I thought it must be important, but I did not really understand what was going on half the time. However, when I entered boarding school all of this disappeared entirely from my mental horizon. Partly it was the absence of sources of news in the school, but more importantly, I think, it was just the sense that nothing "out there" was really relevant anymore. So the Kennedy years in the United States are basically a complete blank in my political memory. At one point a group of Cuban boys arrived at the boarding school who kept shouting about "the Communists," but most of them left again after a single term. Their sudden appearance, I suppose, was part of the fallout of the Bay of Pigs. When I arrived at Columbia, then, after several years of almost complete isolation, the other students all seemed to me tremendously worldly-wise and clued-in about things, as indeed they were compared with me, and they also all seemed politically very well informed—as indeed they were—and self-confident in expressing their views. Sidney Morgenbesser used to say, "At age eighteen Descartes invented analytic geometry all on his own, and this gave him some self-confidence." The other undergraduates whom I encountered seemed to me all to speak as if each one had just invented analytic geometry.

Not long after classes began, I encountered a group of students with placards demonstrating outside the McMillin Theater at 116th Street and Broadway. They were shouting, or rather rhythmically intoning over and over, the words "Vietnam, American Algeria." There were so many demonstrators that they spilled off the pavement and blocked uptown lanes of Broadway completely, so that traffic began to back up. There was also a large crowd of bystanders, and groups of policemen were milling around in a rather random way. The driver of one of the cabs that was stuck in the blockage of the traffic got out of his cab and began to shout loudly "Da finks, da finks," gesturing toward the demonstrators. What did any of this mean? I hadn't a clue. I eventually asked one of the students who was standing there in the crowd what Vietnam had to do with *Algeria,* but he muttered something incomprehensible about "the Dragon Lady." In fact what was in progress was a demonstration against Madame Nhu, called "the Dragon Lady," who was the wife of Ngo Dinh Nhu. Ngo Dinh Nhu was both brother of and chief adviser to the South Vietnamese president, Ngo Dinh Diem. She was about to arrive to give a talk in McMillan Theater. In New York at that time, though, it was not difficult to get information if one wished to, and when a few years later I first saw Gillo Pontecorvo's *La Bataille d'Alger* at the university film club in the same theater, I knew very well why the United States in Vietnam and France in Algeria could be seen as parallels. Later that month Diem was assassinated, a month or so later John F. Kennedy was killed, and then Lee Harvey Oswald (on television).

There was nothing in the real politics of the 1960s in the United States that would have persuaded a young man like me, or anyone who was not already tacitly convinced that liberals were automatically always on the side of the angels, that classic liberalism was a particularly attractive position to adopt. After all, the major political issue was the war in Vietnam, which had been first planned and was now being conducted by people in the Kennedy and Johnson administrations who had reputations as standard-bearers of liberalism. To be sure, when a conservative Republican administration came to power under Nixon, the president continued and intensified the war, but if the best that liberals could cite in their own defense was that the conservatives were just as bad, that was rather weak beer. On the particularly burning structural issue of race, the liberals had perhaps a slightly better record than they did on the war, but they did not seem to be initiating much, merely (at best) responding to forces in the Black community whose aspirations did not necessarily take a liberal form, and were none the worse for that. On a wider range of other social, economic, and political issues, liberalism did not seem to be an ideology that was actively generating either much original thought or much effective practical action. None of this was, perhaps, strictly a "refutation" of liberalism, but, as I said, it also meant that there was nothing terribly inviting about the liberal position.

I had decided I wanted to go to Columbia because I had liked the impression the city made on me and because Krigler advised me to apply. I had no particular expectations about the courses of study on offer. There were plenty of self-described liberals in the university. Lionel Trilling in the Department of English gave his lectures on "Modern Writers" that a lot of students attended, although his theoretical devotion to the liberal imagination seemed to be connected to his fear of imaginary Stalinists who needed to be outmaneuvered, and made him seem just out of touch with reality. I think, too, that the Department of Government (what elsewhere was called Political Science) will have been very densely populated by liberals of various kinds. That, however, was not true of the Department of Philosophy. There were three very substantial figures there who taught political philosophy: Robert Paul Wolff, Sidney Morgenbesser, and Robert Denoon Cumming. All of them were, each in his own way, critics of liberalism from the Left. I admired all three of these philosophers greatly, learned a lot from each of them, and continue, in retrospect, to count myself very fortunate to have encountered them when I did.

CHAPTER 8

Robert Paul Wolff

The Poverty of Liberalism

Und die Gerechtigkeit muß ex officio stockblind sein. Die Allegoriefinder haben ihr die Augen verbunden—warum? Damit sie nicht sieht, wohin sich die Waagschale neigt, und reintun kann, was sie will.

And justice must ex officio be blind as a bat. Those who invent allegories put a bandage over her eyes—why? So that she might not see in which direction the scales are tilting, and can put in the pans whatever she wants.

—Nestroy, *Die schlimmen Buben in der Schule*

ROBERT PAUL WOLFF is now perhaps most closely associated with the book he wrote in the late 1960s entitled *In Defense of Anarchism*.[1] He thought of himself as a Kantian who had discovered that the implications of Kant's views were a form of theoretical anarchism. Anarchists were different from, say, socialists in that socialists were primarily interested in the socioeconomic organization of society, that is, the question of who owned and who controlled what resources, whereas anarchists were primarily interested in questions of usurped authority. Characteristic socialist slogans might include such things as "Property is theft" or "To each according to his need, from each according to his ability," but the anarchists' motto "*Ni dieu ni maître*" didn't directly refer to the economy at all. Rather the anarchist slogan was a rejection of the claims by the church or the state to issue normatively tinged demands for obedience. The "anarchism" Wolff defended was the rejection of Krigler's third sense of "authority" as it was thought to exist in the political sphere, that is, the idea that we have some kind of normative obligation to obey the directives of legitimate governments. We might, Wolff argued, have various reasons to do what a government demanded of us (such as that what it ordered made sense or was reasonable in itself), but these reasons would not include that we (morally) ought to obey what any state demanded, as if it had legitimate authority. No really existing government, he concluded, was legitimate, nor was it possible to imagine any form of collective organization that could satisfy the conditions that would have be fulfilled for the political demands of that organization to be morally binding on individuals, as traditional accounts of "political obligation" would demand.

In calling himself a follower of Kant, Wolff placed himself in a distinguished tradition of people who thought they knew what Kant meant better than he did himself—most notably, Fichte, who said, roughly speaking, that he was just turning the rebarbative Kantian text into something with a little more clarity, organization, and polish. Fichte ended up claiming that the state must foster the freedom of its citizens by distributing property to them, regulating through a system of licenses all economic activity, and providing work for everyone to do. This would require all the borders of the state to be closed to external commerce.[2] The reason for this, he thought, was that in the modern world, universal government regulation of the economy and complete autarchy were the only guarantees that all the individual citizens would always have work and thus could always be active and free.

Kant construed my relation to myself in its moral aspects as a form of self-legislation, or giving myself a universal law for my own action. So an external political process, that of making laws, was imaginatively projected into the *forum internum* of the human soul, in perhaps something like the way in which, in the ancient world, the external political process of deliberation—the Athenian assembly deliberating whether or not to execute the inhabitants of Mytilene—came metaphorically to be applied to the internal thought processes of an individual—Mikrokles deliberating whether or not to buy some sprats in the market. Despite this provenance, it has always seemed to me exceptionally odd that anyone would think that our relation to any political organization could be usefully understood in terms derived from individual morality, even if the individual morality in question had itself been metaphorically reconfigured as being something like a political process. This is particularly true if the political activity which served as a model was the very limited, highly constrained, and artificial process of legislation. Wolff's conclusion in the book is that there is no moral ought involved in our relation to the state, hence that no state is legitimate. While not inclined to deny this conclusion, I suggest that the problems he diagnoses might lie as much in his narrow Kantian ideas about the moral ought per se as in his account of the legitimatory self-presentation of the state. If the moral ought in anything like the form in which Kant envisaged it—or anything like the form in which Wolff thought Kant envisaged it—does not at all exist, then it is not surprising that we have no moral obligations (in the requisite sense) to the state and its laws.

Fun and Games

I became interested in Wolff's views not as a result of *In Defense of Anarchism,* but when, while I was studying for a year in Freiburg im Breisgau, Germany, during 1967–1968, I read an essay he wrote about tolerance. I came across *Kritik der reinen Toleranz,* a translation into German of a book which contained three essays, one by Herbert Marcuse which later became very well known (at least for a while in some circles), one by a Harvard historian named Barrington Moore, and the third by Wolff.[3] I don't remember much about it, apart from Wolff's treatment of an issue which was, I think, only marginally connected to the ostensible topic (tolerance). That issue was the desire on the part of proponents of some forms of liberalism to find a fully neutral or impartial framework that all could, despite great differences in their substantive views, interests, and values, agree on as the final normative matrix of politics. If such a framework could be found, it would not have to be imposed by force (presumably because everyone could agree on it), and so this would make it particularly attractive to liberals.

Wolff began by saying that one suggestion for a framework was the equal and impartial enforcement of a single set of rules, the same for all, but that a moment's reflection would suffice to see that this was at any rate not sufficient to ensure even anything like what we would call "justice," much less to ensure that a society in which it was instantiated would be acceptable in other more general ways. Thus, if you had a twenty-year-old boy boxing with, or competing in a running competition with, a twelve-year-old boy, you would quickly notice that the twenty-year-old almost always won. This would not be any less true if one installed an impartial judge who enforced some simple and plausible set of rules that were "the same [equal] for all."

These might be rules such as, in the case of running, that everyone started at the same time from the same place at the starter's signal, and no one could trip up another runner. In boxing they might be rules like no hitting below the belt, no wearing of any special protective gear, and no use of brass knuckles. There isn't much doubt but that the strict enforcement of these rules would introduce a kind of predictable regularity and equality into the games, but we all also know what else would happen. Surprise! In most cases the twenty-year-old boy would still win, the reason being simply that twenty-year-old boys are generally stronger and quicker than twelve-year-old boys are. The same would usually also be the case if one pitted a twenty-year-old who weighed 45 kilos against one who weighed 60 kilos.

Something similar might be observed in other situations, too. Consider, for instance, the following possible case: there are some very wealthy owners of a factory who could easily afford to keep it idle for a month without more than a moderate loss of income, which they don't by any stretch of the imagination "need" to continue to lead a perfectly comfortable life, and then there are the workers in the factory whose families, in the event of enforced unemployment for a month, would be very seriously pinched, even if they might not strictly starve. Suppose now that these two groups are in conflict about working conditions or pay. Enforcing simple, equal rules on both parties, impartially, such as that negotiations would take place for three hours in the morning and three in the afternoon every day until agreement was reached, would have a predictable outcome. The owners would drag out the negotiations until the workers became so desperate or destitute that they had no choice but to accept virtually any *diktat* that was imposed on them. This would then count as "fair" and justified, perhaps even "freely agreed on," certainly "consented to," if one's standard was that of impartial enforcement of these "equal" rules.

The cases considered were ones in which there existed gross disparity in power between the two parties in question—the power to run and box in the case of the boys; the power to survive and continue to live a minimally decent life in the case of the owners and the workers. Enforcing equal rules in cases in which gross disparities of power exist will not only not automatically abolish pre-existing differences in power, but can have the effect of reinforcing them, rendering them more stable and permanent or even increasing them. To see why enforced "equality" may *increase* disparities in power, imagine that access to university (and then subsequently to various desirable careers) is made contingent on winning a boxing match. There is nothing inherently or formally incoherent about that. It is not excluded by some law of impartiality; the judges of the boxing match may be perfectly impartial.

At this point the reader is likely to say, "Ah, but it isn't *fair* to pit scrawny twelve-year-olds who have never boxed before against well nourished and extensively trained twenty-year-olds. This is why there are complex regulations to take systematic account of differences. Thus, there was instituted a system of weight classes so that boxers competed only against those of more or less equal general physique, and there were phenomena such as handicaps and head starts given to younger runners who were matched against older ones." The reader might then go on to say, "Introducing these restrictions and this system of handicaps and head starts merely means that we are 'making the playing field level' *before* the competition. Once the playing field is level, impartial enforcement of a series of simple equal rules is all that is required."

This looks like it saves the general idea of impartiality via enforcement of a system of equal rules. One just needs to add a few further rules, such as that competition is only between boys of more or less the same age. However, the crucial fact is that to know what corrections to introduce into the system of rules one needs concrete, but also relatively ad hoc, knowledge of the real world, and one has to know how to apply that so as to get something like what we call a level playing field. This means knowing that age and weight are relevant factors in boxing, so you don't pit a twelve-year-old who weighs 45 kilos against a twenty-year-old who weighs 60 kilos. However, it also means knowing that, for instance, the color of one's eyes is not relevant to the outcome of a boxing match, nor the astrological sign that was dominant at the moment of one's birth, so they do not require correction or compensation. Who decides what counts as a relevant antecedent difference? How about if you pit thirteen-year-old boys of the same weight who have been starved against thirteen-year-old boys of the same weight who are well nourished and have been systematically trained to run or box? Which drugs can be used by a competitor fairly and which are to be prohibited?

Extrapolating here one will see that several issues arise. First, will you actually get everyone to agree about what counts as a relevant factor, and would not the absence of agreement about that vitiate the further and more general claims which liberalism might wish to make about the adequacy of this framework? How far are you willing to go in correcting for irregularities in the field of play? Robert Paul Wolff cited *The Rise of the Meritocracy* as a book that represented a kind of *reductio ad absurdum* of this approach.[4] I later realized that this was just an instance of Marx's general view that absolute equality was an illusion.[5]

Even if one abstracts from the fact that absolute equality is a conceptual impossibility and a very destructive actual practical goal, and locates relative equality in a concrete political context, there seems something rather arbitrary about it. The more you introduce various corrections (handicaps, etc.), the closer you come to a point at which it seems that you are not impartially following the rules for equality but are revising the rules ad hoc to get the result you think you ought to get. Where this process starts and where it ends is arbitrary. Why consider *this* as a potentially relevant factor and not *that*? Why does discussion end at *this* point?

Lectio Difficilior

When we decide to introduce new measures to level the playing field, this is a bit like a procedure I knew from school when learning Latin. We were told that we needed to avoid "taking the Latin from the sense rather than the sense from the Latin." That is, we boys who did not know Latin at all well were tempted to help ourselves by projecting what we assumed the passage *must* be trying to say on to the text and then using that as a crib to extract exactly that sense again, regardless of what the Latin actually said. This distinction between taking the Latin from the meaning rather than the meaning from the Latin will not stand up to scrutiny, if pressed and taken absolutely strictly. As various hermeneuticists have pointed out, if one really had no idea whatever of what was supposed to be in a text, one would not be able to make any sense of it at all.[6] At least one must assume it is written in Latin (and in something like proper Latin, Latin not too deformed to be at all comprehensible). With this comment we are back in the territory marked out by the incoherence of *sola scriptura*.

Absolutely presuppositionless understanding is, as the proponents of hermeneutics point out, completely impossible. They, however, also then hasten to point out that this is perfectly compatible with the existence of real processes of understanding. It is merely the case that understanding requires one to assimilate and initially proceed by adopting a pre-existing network of assumptions. This is called "entering the hermeneutic circle." If all goes well, once one is inside, one can revise the initial assumptions. Inside that web, in the *local* context, the distinction between taking the Latin from the sense rather than taking the sense from the Latin not only makes sense, but making and observing this distinction is indispensable if one is to learn anything new from what one reads. It is the basis of one of the recognized principles of textual criticism: *lectio difficilior,* which essentially recommends that if there are two readings of a passage, one containing a more unfamiliar word, or a word used in a more unfamiliar construction, and the other with a very frequently used word, used in a familiar way, the former is to be preferred. Scribes, it is assumed, would have been unlikely to introduce unnecessary difficulty into a text they are copying, but would have been more like, unconsciously or even consciously, to change the unusual to something more familiar. One could see something like the application of *lectio difficilior* in Krigler's treatment of scandalous contradictions in biblical texts. "Choose the more difficult reading" is, of course, not an infallible rule; sometimes scribes did just have a lapse and write nonsense. One does not choose the more difficult reading if it really makes no sense at all (but is a simple scribal mistake), and so "more difficult" really means "more unusual but still, perhaps just barely, possible." Sometimes this requires the reader to expand his or her own understanding of what is possible / comprehensible; when that happens there is a distinct cognitive (and probably also moral) gain. To make that judgment, however—"this is highly unusual, but just barely possible"—requires a rather high level of competence in the language, lots of experience, and usually also some imagination. There is no algorithm or guarantee here. "How do you know you have not just projected the meaning you assume must be there onto that text?" has as its parallel "How do you know you are not artificially imposing the result you think must be right by fiddling with the initial conditions for a level playing field?"

Rawls

When I came back to New York in September 1968, I made a point of going to Wolff's lectures. The basic components of the criticism of liberalism that I heard in his lectures during that period in the mid-1960s are formulated in the book which he published in 1968, *The Poverty of Liberalism*.[7] I won't recount the points he makes in that book here, but I was very impressed with his proleptic criticism of John Rawls. I say "proleptic" because this was before the definitive version of the theory was even published. Wolff had been a student at Harvard, and had access to a lot of material by Rawls before it appeared in print, through circulated early drafts and reports from students. He was thus able to discuss Rawls's central views even before *A Theory of Justice* came out in 1971.[8]

Rawls, Wolff said, was an ideological genius because he showed how one could argue from accepted liberal premises to the "justice" of gross forms of social and economic inequality. It was important to see that the justification of real inequality was the actual effect, if not the intention, of his position. Its basic claim was: "Many apparently egregious inequalities can actually be defended as *just* on the ground that without them those who are worst off would be even worse off." To give an example, assume that A has $100 million income each year, whereas B has $20,000 a year. How could this be considered to be just?

The trick was to make one's immediate reaction to this *not* be outrage, and this was done by claiming that this result—it is *just* that A has so much more than B—"really" was an expression of a deep equality, invisible to the human eye until Rawls brought it out. Rawls argues for this by inventing an imaginary situation—"the original position"—and populating it with imaginary agents who are postulated to be equal, and also not to know anything about their own empirical identity or their actual state of wealth or position in society. Then, he argues that such imaginary agents in such an original position would agree on a set of rules. One of these rules, he claimed, was that unlimited real inequality was justified, provided it was necessary to improve the wellbeing of those least well off. If you could then get real people to identify with these imaginary agents, you had your case won. So in the example given in the previous paragraph, this unequal distribution between A and B was justified, provided the following counterfactual was true: Assume that B is the least well-off member of the society, then if A were to have less, B would also have less. That is, for instance, If A were to have only $99 million, then B would have only $19,000. This is supposed to be fair and just because it follows from a set of rules which we—or rather our imaginary representatives—would all freely agree on.

Once one had internalized Wolff's way of seeing Rawls's basic insight, one would not be at all impressed by any of the increasingly complex epicycles that were added to the theory. Rawls had filled a major gap that existed in American ideology, and he filled it to a tee, by providing a theory which permitted a population deeply committed to massive *real* inequality to feel good about themselves, because the obscene differences in wealth, power, and life-chances in their society were mere surface phenomena, which anyone with a deep under-standing would see were really just expressions of profound human equality. The inequality is real and palpable; the equality an added imaginary construct. Wolff diagnosed this as just the latest version of the difficulty which Marx had pointed out in Rousseau: the equality Rousseau ascribes to people was that of the imaginary citizen, whereas the inequality he left effectively unaddressed was that of the real em-pirical persons, and the former was in some sense to justify the latter.[9]

Anarchism

I was very positively impressed with Wolff's criticisms of liberal con-ceptions of toleration and ideas of neutrality and fairness, but there was still something about his "anarchism" which I couldn't accept for reasons I could not really at the time put my finger on. The basic source of my discomfort, I thought, was that in *In Defense of Anar-chism*, Wolff sets up the issue of political legitimacy as one of recon-ciling the political authority of the group with individual autonomy, and he treats this way of proceeding as if it were something too com-monsensical to question. He then argues to what he presents as the startling conclusion that (roughly) none of the existing forms of po-litical association is actually compatible with "individual autonomy," and draws from that the conclusion that no state structure is legiti-mate. However, this seemed to me to be disingenuous. "Individual autonomy" was just a technical term for our liberal old friend the sov-ereign subject under one of his descriptions, and it was not at all surprising that this subject turned out not to be compatible with var-ious political structures. It was a bit like what Hegel says about Kant's *Ding an sich:* it should be no surprise to discover that we know nothing about it, because it is specifically set up and defined so as to be free of all potential cognitive content. The real question for me was, "Why be so daft as to start from this quasi-Kantian conception of 'individual autonomy' at all? If you do start from that assumption, you have no one but yourself to blame if you end up nowhere." Wolff, I took it, found it inconceivable that one might simply not adopt or accept something like the conception of "individual moral autonomy" which one finds in Kant (and also liberalism) as absolutely fundamental. That, however, seemed to me wrong. Despite his appropriation of a (kind of) Marxist approach to economics, and his self-characterization as an "anarchist," Wolff was in this domain actually something very much like a liberal.

Part of the difficulty here is that there are, in fact, two very different kinds of position, each of which calls itself "anarchist." First, there is libertarian anarchism in the style of Max Stirner.[10] Here each person is encouraged to start with himself as a unique, potentially incomparably wonderful individual, and "egoist," who (purportedly) stands completely on his own two feet, needing no one else, and whose basic relations with the world (and with himself) are those of the ownership of property. No one (and nothing) has any claims on me that are binding. The radical rejection of any form of transcendence has as its complement complete self-centeredness: thus, "*Mir geht nichts über Mich*" (Nothing is more to me than myself) leads to the claim that "*Ich beziehe alles auf Mich*" (I refer everything to myself).[11]

The second position that is called "anarchist" is that of, say, Kropotkin, which we might call communist anarchism.[12] The basic fact of human life for Kropotkin is not the possible existence of some isolated individual who has a sense of the absolute importance of his self-consciousness, autonomy, and moral conceptions. Rather, humans are cultural animals who are always born as members of and live in communities which are held together by natural bonds of mutual aid. Human history should be seen as the story of ways in which those bonds of cooperation are strengthened and the ways in which they are weakened or perverted. The state and private property are rejected because they interfere with beneficial forms of mutual aid and free sociability. The bonds of mutual aid, however, no matter how strained and distorted, are never, in cases that are not pathological exceptions, dissolved completely. The "ego" of Descartes, Locke, Kant, and Stirner is a conceptual abstraction which misses the point. If you really want to understand the human world at any given point in time, look at the characteristic forms of reciprocity and social cooperation in the major groups; they are what hold the society together and make it able to survive and are thus preconditions for the existence of any given individual. Subjectivity, consciousness, the individual ego, the sovereign self are not basic or free-standing phenomena. Individual humans, to be sure, may reflect in different subjective ways on the forms of mutual aid on which they depend, they may fail (or actively refuse) to acknowledge some of them, they may act in various ways so as to free themselves from real dependency on them. These are all secondary and derivative.

Unless these two very different forms of anarchism are clearly distinguished and kept separate, nothing but the greatest confusion will result. While liberals can find some common ground with the libertarian form of anarchism, the communist version would have to be anathema to them. Looked at from this point of view, Wolff's libertarian anarchism was just a form of liberalism that got out of control.

CHAPTER 9

Sidney Morgenbesser

Philosophy as Practical Surrealism

From any proposition or the negation of any proposition draw the conclusion: therefore God exists.

—First principle of Jewish logic, according to
Sidney Morgenbesser

If *p*, why not *q*?

—Second principle of Jewish logic, according to
Sidney Morgenbesser

THE TEACHER I ENCOUNTERED at Columbia who had overall the greatest influence on me was Sidney Morgenbesser, but he, who seemed keenly engaged by almost anything else, was not theoretically at all interested in liberalism. At any rate, it was a topic that never seemed to come up in conversation, and if it did somehow come up, the discussion always moved on and veered away from "liberalism" as a general concept. I must say that I never noticed this at the time; I am only recognizing it now in retrospect as I think back on those days with the specific intention of focusing on this topic. However, now that I think of it, it does seem to me to warrant mention. Perhaps the strongest anti-liberal message Sidney could have sent me was just the obvious absence of the whole phenomenon from any conversation he ever had with me.

Sidney's whole life was discussion, and most of it was public discussion. He was, as it were, all out-front there all the time; his motor was always running, the gears engaged; the gleaming constantly shifting dialectical surface was uninterruptedly rotating. Walking down the street with him elicited a constant stream of witty, incisive, apt comments, observations, and remarks on all aspects of the passing show (in addition to general comments on philosophical theses, bits of Jewish lore, and random reminiscences of life on the Lower East Side). I had never seen and heard, and have never since seen or heard, anything like it: one would have paid for admission. Sidney really never stopped: I once visited him in the closed psychiatric ward of the New York hospital where he was confined for a course of electroshock treatments for depression, only to find him conducting something that was a mixture of a talk show and a seminar with a huge group of other patients, visitors, and members of staff, who clustered around listening to him with rapt attention.

Sidney had a very keen appreciation of something which it was difficult for most versions of liberalism to accommodate, and that was the existence of groups who felt themselves to have essential identities. He raised this when talking about some highly traditionalist Jewish groups. For them it was not that they were composed of sovereign individuals who had all chosen to identify with the group, but that their members were to some extent born with an identity which they could not be and were not supposed even to imagine themselves as distanced from. Even to imagine themselves in the aboriginal situation of liberalism, as free sovereign choosers, was in some sense itself already wrong. You could talk to them until you were blue in the face and would never convince them in discussion. If you changed their form of life radically, intervening in it and disturbing it at its very roots—for instance by kidnapping their children and subjecting them to a completely different set of practices—then, of course, that was something else, but you would never get their free consent to that. To this, all the liberal could say, Sidney thought, was that they shouldn't *be* like that, which was perhaps true, but a very odd thing for a liberal to say.

This did not at all surprise me because I had heard something like this—not exactly the same story because embellished with various in-vocations of "free will"—from Krigler about Catholicism.

Sidney and the Waitress

Sidney had an inimitably ludic way of engaging in the criticism of a position. Sometimes, he would simply tell a joke, for instance, when the university administration designated Professor X from the Department of Economics to review allocation of space in the Department of Philosophy. Professor X reported that the departmental common room was "underutilized" in the afternoons and could be reassigned to another department. Sidney proposed that we write to Professor X to the effect that we had observed that his living room was "underutilized in the afternoons" when his wife sat around in it doing nothing and that we proposed to have it reassigned to us.[1]

Sometimes Sidney would execute proper skits of the kind one would expect from performance art, or a book of surrealist party games. The whole thing could look like a slightly odd practical joke. Thus, Sidney once went into Chock Full O'Nuts, a coffee shop that used to exist on the south side of 116th St between Broadway and River-side Drive. This shop offered not just coffee but pastries, including deeply disgusting donuts. Sidney, however, liked them. The very resigned-looking waitress obviously knew what to expect from him, as in fact I think most people on Morningside Heights did by that time because he was a familiar figure, so she began:

WAITRESS: What can I bring you? You want donuts?

SIDNEY: What kind of donuts do you have?

WAITRESS: Today we have vanilla and chocolate.

SIDNEY: I'll have vanilla.

WAITRESS: Now that I think of it, we may also have some jelly donuts in the back.

SIDNEY: OK, I'll have a vanilla donut, except if you have jelly donuts in the back, I'll have chocolate.

The battle-hardened waitress, who had probably in the past suffered much worse than this at Sidney's hands, wearily went off to get him his donut. This, of course, was Sidney's way of refuting the axiom of the independence of irrelevant alternatives, originally formulated by Kenneth Arrow in his paper on rational choice theory.[2] The idea is that a person's preference between, say, vanilla and chocolate, is supposed to be fixed and independent of the presence of any other possible choice (jelly donut). Since obviously much of politics depends on strategic decisions about the formatting of political choices, defining what was and what was not relevant, and imposing this on others, this axiom had never seemed to me of much use, but Sidney preferred to go for the jugular.[3] Robert Paul Wolff in a related discussion used an overtly political example. Suppose I am presented with an electoral choice between a moderately right-of-center party

(R) and a moderately left-of-center party (L). I may under those circumstances distinctly prefer L. Suppose now that a properly fascist party (F) puts forward a candidate. It might well be the case that I prefer party L over party R, if that is the choice, but if there is a serious threat from party F, I would prefer party R over party L, because, for instance, I think R would be able to be more effective in cracking down and undermining the fascists than L would be.[4]

Sidney and the Lawyer

The episode at Chock Full O'Nuts was not perhaps a direct criticism of liberalism except to the extent to which the rational decision theory which Arrow practiced had a kind of affinity to the idea of the sovereign individual chooser of the liberal tradition. Sidney, however, executed a further performance that was more directly focused on a central tenet of liberalism (among other positions); it concerned one of the consequences of the events of 1968 at Columbia, events which I did not witness directly myself because I was in Germany during the whole of 1967–1968. The outlines of what happened, though, are not subject to much disagreement: protesting students occupied some university buildings, and when the officials of the university administration threatened to call the police, a group of members of the teaching staff formed a picket line as a *cordon sanitaire* around some of the occupied buildings. The idea was that the New York City police were obviously completely willing to assault students, but might be unlikely to use excessive force against university teachers. This turned out to be a miscalculation because the police rioted and assaulted first the teachers, and then the students in the buildings. Sidney, who was on the picket line, was one of those beaten by the police. He was said to have worn a large bandage on his head—which he called his "brain-drain"—for several days after being released from hospital. Some years later, Sidney was called for jury duty and interrogated by some of the court officers who were trying to exclude from consideration jurors who had prejudicial attitudes. It was a case of purported police brutality, so the court officer asked Sidney whether he had himself ever had any unpleasant or unfair experiences with the police. Sidney thought for a moment and replied that he had had an unpleasant experience—being beaten up by the police in 1968—but he couldn't really say it was unfair because the police were beating everybody up on that occasion. This has always seemed to me a characteristically pithy insight into the inherent superficiality of any approach to human societies that gives too much centrality to fairness.

Some people spoke and wrote as if they thought that conceptions of fairness were natural, universal, or invariant among humans. However, they are anything but "natural" and universal. Suppose a mother is cutting a cake and gives child A a much bigger piece than she gives child B, or suppose that child A takes child B's piece in addition to his own. Now in that case, it might well be right that child B will cause a fuss. If one wants, one can call that a "natural" reaction, but there is a huge, socially mediated step from that reaction to the claim that the reason child B is upset is that he feels he has been unfairly treated. If one cat takes food away from another, the second may make a fuss, but no one would attribute to the cat a natural sense of fairness. Child B may be upset because he lost his cake or because he wants more cake than he has, but he needs to be taught and to learn to say "That's not fair" as a way of getting more cake, and he can do that only if the vocabulary of fairness exists in his language and if conceptions of fairness are widely entrenched in the surrounding society, and we know that this is not the case. Just as we know that many societies lack any conception of universal human equality, but rather *assume* that slaves and free persons, men and women, members of the in-group and foreigners are obviously not equal and should not be treated equally, so many societies simply lack our highly specific concept of "fairness." So one would be extremely ill advised to treat it blithely as an unproblematic and unquestioned assumption in any philosophical argument.

Sidney, Robert Paul Wolff, and the Oxford Dons

Both Robert Paul Wolff and Sidney had a very low opinion of early and mid-twentieth-century Oxford moral philosophy. Wolff had studied at Oxford for a while—this must have been in the late fifties—and was basically revolted by what he saw as the scholasticism of the ethics that was done there. There was, as far as he could tell, no real disagreement at all among Oxford philosophers about what ethics required of us. They differed from each other on only two minor practical points: whether we had duties toward animals and whether it was permissible to commit suicide. The study of ethics was reduced to simply searching for more and more arcane and clever arguments for a conclusion that was taken to be fixed from the very beginning, that is, for proving that people should not lie, should not steal, and should pay their taxes. This was the same structure Sidney had analyzed for "Jewish logic": the conclusion (that God exists) was given from the start, and, as Sidney put it, "thinking" consisted of inventing more and complex arguments for this conclusion and refutations of proposed counterarguments.

The reader might be unconvinced by Wolff's objections to Oxford ethics on two grounds. First of all, one might think that differences about how to act toward animals and about the attitude one should take toward suicide are not really as trivial as Wolff seemed to make out that they were. At the start of the *Myth of Sisyphus,* Camus claims that the question of suicide is the only genuine philosophical question, and even if one thinks that that is an exaggeration, suicide is surely an important and legitimate topic for reflection and discussion. The same is true of our relation to the natural world, in particular to animals. This reaction is, I think, wrong because Wolff was not denying the importance of these topics, but rather rejecting the constricting format that was thought to be the only one in which discussion of them could be couched. Was it inevitable that we must think about humans and animals only in the categories of utility, duty, or rights? Was "permission or prohibition" the only thing to discuss about suicide? Was it through putting the question in this way that one could approach the most interesting aspects of our relation to our own death?

Second, one might think that the structure Wolff described—knowing the conclusion you wanted to come to and then trying to invent an argument for it—was not self-evidently a recipe for scholasticism, but actually something more like a description of an important strand in almost all human thought. Wolff himself in other contexts emphasized that philosophers did not, in general, pluck some arbitrary, or even apparently well-supported, assumptions out of the air and then simply explore the logical consequences of these assumptions, eventually reaching conclusions which they then automatically and wholeheartedly embraced because of their overwhelming rationality. Thinking was always trying to get somewhere and so there had to be some sense of a possible goal, a conclusion one was trying to reach, for anything to happen at all. Philosophers always knew the conclusion they wanted to reach before starting the argument although, if they were any good, they could also be surprised by what they discovered in the course of the argument and even change their minds. He illustrated this in his own case. He had started thinking about the argument which he eventually presented in the book *In Defense of Anarchism* because he thought he could find a positive solution to what he took to be the basic problem of political philosophy: how political obligation could be made compatible with individual moral autonomy. He was sure there was an argument for this, because without it political philosophy and, he thought, contemporary political life were in some sense without foundations. He was, therefore, very strongly motivated to find that argument. This was the only reason he undertook the project. However, in his own particular case, although he tried everything he could think of to find a "justification" for political obligation, he eventually had to recognize that all the arguments he could come up with failed, and he had the moral courage to accept that and reverse the conclusion. Instead of *In Defense of Political Obligation* he wrote *In Defense of Anarchism*. I, of course, thought he should have drawn a completely different conclusion, namely that the reason the argument failed was the liberal idea of moral autonomy with which he started, but his ability to change his mind as a result of argumentation was still impressive. To apply this to Wolff's views about Oxford, then, it wasn't that Oxford philosophers were all trying to justify existing British middle-class morality; what else would you expect them to be doing? Rather it was that they did not seem ever to be able or willing to follow out any of the implications of their arguments that in any way threw doubt on the central tenets of their way of life. This was what was unphilosophical.

Sidney's direct dealings with people at Oxford were much more limited, amounting only to an extended visit or two, but he was equally repelled by the atmosphere there. The dons welcomed him, but did so in a way that seemed to him objectionable. They acted, he said, as if they were doing him a great favor by accepting him into their common room, and did so because he made them laugh. He had become somewhat sensitive to being seen as an entertainer rather than a serious thinker, but more importantly he sensed behind the acceptance a great willingness to use, if it suited them, the power of exclusion which this group of people had, and this disturbed him. This, one could say, was a mere personal reaction of his with no special cognitive standing, but Sidney also had another complaint which was more substantial, and similar to the kinds of things Wolff said, although expressed in Sidney's typical ludic manner. People at Oxford, he said, seemed to think that every man was born with an innate knowledge of the rules of cricket, and thus with the idea of fair play. This, however, was a very poor starting point for understanding anything about the world. Thus, when it came to their attention that most people in most countries did not observe these rules, and, even worse, had no idea that they existed, Oxford moral philosophers did not modify their views, but simply wrote the rest of the world off as perverse. However, Sidney said, they ought to have taken to heart Locke's criticism of the doctrine of innate ideas, and recognized that not even the idea of fairness is part of the apparatus of thought which everyone is born with.

Sidney and Motivation

In a way the most important thing I learned from Sidney was something intangible about how it was possible and appropriate to proceed in philosophy. Sidney made a clear distinction between two different dimensions involved in our dealings with philosophical theories, views, or positions. On the one hand, there was the dimension of evidence and reasoning, which encompassed a number of potentially different things, all, however, connected in one way or another with the marshalling of empirical or argumentative support for a position or theory. This might include collecting apparent observational evidence for the theory, giving arguments for it, trying to show how it can explain various otherwise incomprehensible phenomena, developing and elaborating it in various ways, and rebutting criticisms of it. Traditionally philosophy put these matters in the very center of its attention; discussing them was the bread and butter of the traditional philosophic craft as usually practiced, and so most of them have been very thoroughly canvassed and treated.

Sidney, however, insisted that there was another dimension to our relation to philosophical or theoretical approaches and positions that was much more closely connected with questions of human psychology and motivation. One can perfectly reasonably ask about, say, "the arguments that have been given" for or against utilitarianism, monotheism, or mind-brain reductionism, but also about the relation which some individual, say, Jane, entertains to those positions (and to the mass of philosophical argumentation surrounding them). Thus, appropriate questions here might be such things as: "Does she believe in this theory (reductionism or utilitarianism or what have you)?" "Is she engaged in serious consideration of it and the arguments for and against it?" "Is she (now) motivated to continue to discuss, elaborate, or defend it?" "Is she committed to it? (in what way?)" "Is she willing to use it? Under what circumstances and how is she willing to use it?" Obviously these are all slightly different things. I can use a theory without in some sense believing in it—it is just a rough rule of thumb or means of calculation—and I can continue to engage in defending a theory with arguments even if I don't in some sense believe it and would never use it as a guide when I need to act. Many philosophers have devoted some attention to these questions, but Sidney thought that all too often the discussion was still slightly overshadowed by a set of naive assumptions. The most important of these was the tacit expectation that a fully rational person's motives, commitments, and engagements would track the course of "the argument" in a simple and easily discernible way. If a rational person is given more evidence and increasingly better arguments for some view or position, she increasingly comes—or at any rate should come—to believe that that view is correct, and to act on it; engagement and commitment should follow the evidence in the other direction, too, so that as the evidentiary and argumentative tide turns against a view, this should be visibly mapped in the way in which a rational person distances herself from it. Of course, in fact, this is not what usually happens, but most philosophers thought that that is, in a sense, philosophically unimportant, a mere matter of the empirical failure of most humans to live up to ideal standards of rationality.

If this were a fully correct analysis of the situation, Sidney asserted, then our almost exclusive concentration on the "argument," the evidence, the reasoning, the first of the two dimensions, would be understandable, because it would be the case that everything in the second dimension ought ideally to depend on what happened in the first dimension. Sidney, of course, would never have thought of denying that it was in general a very good idea to be guided in one's beliefs, engagements, and actions by the evidence. One would have to be a fool to deny this. However, he did not think that this general principle told the whole story. Many kinds of action and belief did not actually fit this scheme in any very straightforward way. There were many significant cases where commitment ran ahead of evidence or engagement lagged behind, or in which people turned away from and simply lost motivation to pursue theories that had not really been refuted. One could claim, if one wished, that all cases like this were just instances of human weakness or irrationality, but was this really a plausible or helpful way to proceed? Suppose Jane had followed with great care all the evidentiary and argumentative moves in the discussion of Ptolemaic astronomy, utilitarianism, monotheism, or mind-brain reductionism. Suppose also that she came to the conclusion that these positions had not been refuted and perhaps had as much support as the obvious alternatives. Suppose finally that she then distanced herself from one of these theories, or stopped using it as a guide for action, and failed to bother to defend it in discussion, as she had, perhaps, previously done. To say at that point that her loss of engagement was a merely psychological phenomenon about which the philosopher had nothing more to say was more than simply disappointing; it was an abdication.

The two dimensions, while never, at least in the case of sane people, being completely disengaged, were not really identical, and philosophy ought to have something to say about both of them, and about their possible modes of interaction. Sidney did not claim to have himself a considered global theory, here, but he thought that the absence of a theory did not mean that it was not an important, and viable, task to think seriously about these issues. In this context he had us read John Henry Newman's *Grammar of Assent*, which is about the relation of faith and reason. This was, to say the least, a text I had not expected to encounter in an undergraduate philosophy course at Columbia.

The basic experience I had in reading Newman was that he and I were on the same path, but moving in precisely opposite directions. He was keen to show that it was not irrational to believe things on faith although there was no real rational support for them, and I wanted to say that the Catholicism represented by Krigler and Senje was not internally incoherent and there was no specifiable argument that it seemed to me to have lost, but nevertheless I was not motivated or inclined to accept it. A proper Catholic would say that I had "lost the faith," but this is a theoretically highly charged description of the situation which I would not accept, if only because it seemed to presuppose that I had "had the faith" to start with. I did finally began to wonder whether the reason Sidney didn't talk much about liberalism was not that he thought there was some knock-down argument against it, but that he had thought about it for a long time, and, although he never said anything to this effect, he simply found he lacked motivation to engage with it on its own terms any more.

CHAPTER 10

Robert Denoon Cumming

Human Nature and History

διὰ τὸ μηδεμίαν ἑτοιμότεραν εἶναι τοῖς ἀνθρώποις διόρθωσιν τῆς τῶν προγεγενημένων πράξεων ἐπιστήμης

Because there is nothing more handy for use in correcting people than the knowledge of the actions of those who went before us.

—Polybios, *Histories* 1.1

DESPITE MY GREAT admiration for Sidney Morgenbesser, he was clearly a man of the living and spoken word, not of the written word. He was too intellectually impatient to work over a written text again and again to get the structure and form of expression exactly right. A doctoral dissertation, however, had to be a longish completed, and preferably polished, text, and I worried about my own strength of character and ability to settle on, stay with, and complete an appropriate piece of writing under Sidney's consistently

acute, but also constantly wandering dialectic. The vertiginous kalei-
doscope that was Sidney's mind and discourse was in a way a model
of intellectual activity, as a kind of permanent theoretical motion,
but I thought it was probably also important to be able to take a
snapshot of the provisional results of that activity at some given time
and fix it in writing, even if one's thoughts in some sense really had
already moved on. I thought Sidney, as a doctoral supervisor, would be
an active hindrance to that part of the process. In addition, I wanted
to write something on Heidegger, and Sidney had a complete blind
spot, which he himself acknowledged, about Heidegger. So I turned
to Robert Denoon Cumming and asked him if he would supervise
my dissertation. He was the final teacher at Columbia who influenced me greatly. I hear only too clearly the resounding silence
which greets the mention of his name. He was, even during his life-
time, virtually unknown to the wider public, and for that matter to
most mainstream philosophers, and has now been more or less completely forgotten. I note that his first book, *Human Nature and History,* has been out of print for a while.[1] That he and his work were
and have remained obscure is the result of a combination of factors,
of which his personality and the kind of life he decided to live was
one.

J. S. Mill and the Cross of Lorraine

Bob was a man who belonged to two worlds: New England and
France, or, to put this in more academic terms: Anglo-American political theory and phenomenology-and-existentialism. He had studied
classics at Harvard before the war, but had then gone to France and
Germany for further study. He once told me that one of the crucial
experiences in his life had been wandering down a country lane in

East Anglia after the fall of France and encountering an armored car with the Cross of Lorraine on it, stuck in a hedgerow. He immediately decided to join the Free French and eventually became a liaison officer, responsible for combat intelligence, for General Leclerc's 2nd Armored Division, and received several military decorations.

He was a completely introverted, solitary, self-effacing presence, or perhaps I should say non-presence. He never went to conferences or gave invited talks; he didn't hang out, hobnob, or kibbitz in the way Sidney did everywhere with anyone and everyone. Bob had his lectures and the (large) books which he wrote with extreme care, great deliberation, and very slowly. He was a man of few words; I liked him.

Sidney himself commented on the contrast: "I am a Jew; I play basketball with whoever happens to be around. Bob is a New England Protestant; he plays basketball only with God alone." At this point, Sidney looked at me—pointedly I thought—and said, "So what about you, which are you?" This was a structurally very uncomfortable question for me. Obviously I wasn't a Jew and it would have been not only false but culturally preposterous to say I was a Protestant. So I said to him that he could be perfectly happy as an atheist Jew because his *minyan,* consisting of anybody who happened to be around, was to all intents and purposes self-sufficient, but it was hard to play basketball against an imaginary entity whom you knew to be imaginary unless you had the proper formation for it, which I didn't. If you didn't have that, the game quickly degenerated into something like trying to play tennis without the net. Sidney knew this as well as I did; he was just enjoying himself, waiting to see what I would say.

What I was tempted to add was that I rejected the binary choice. Catholics, even Senje, who wished to "dare to be different," didn't in general like ad hoc scratch groups of players or individual, fully imaginary contests. They preferred to be "different" members of *organized* teams in real encounters (if possible with established practices, sacraments, rituals, and traditions). For "teams" substitute "religious orders," "confraternities," "sodalities," "political parties," "movements" (if sufficiently organized), "schools," etc. However, what was one to do if no acceptable already organized team was in existence which was at all responsive to the actual situation, and yet it was obvious that something new needed to be done—although what that was was not itself clear? No problem for the Jew or Protestant, for obvious reasons. I resisted the temptation to make this additional response. Part of the reason for that stemmed from my reaction to the only occasion on which I heard Herbert Marcuse speak; it was at Columbia in New York in about 1970. At the end of his talk a mischievous member of the audience asked him what political party he supported, and he replied, "Show me a progressive mass working-class political party and I will support it." This did not go down at all well with the audience, who were sophisticated enough to know that this was an elegant way of saying "At the moment, none." It was in fact a feeble answer—perhaps realistic, but certainly feeble—and everyone knew it. My suppressed answer to Sidney would have been equally feeble. Unfortunately, as the seventies progressed, Western economies began to stagnate and we entered the period of political reaction which still persists. As Reagan and Thatcher took over and Rawls began suddenly to be read very assiduously, the changed historical situation transformed what was a form of weakness into something that might look like prescience.

There were, however, other reasons for Bob's failure to attract attention that had to do not with his retiring personality but with the fact that his work was very austere, complex, erudite, and highly unfashionable in its approach. In the 1950s and 1960s he had taught a course entitled "History of Political Theory in Its Institutional Setting" in the Government Department. He had done this with Franz Neumann, who had, at an earlier point in his life, been an associate of the Frankfurt School. It is worth noting that it was, I think, unusual to have a course like this in the United States at that time. Political theory was in general treated as a rather abstract subject, ideally (or perhaps I should say aspirationally) like geometry or chemistry, not as an expression of and reaction to concrete historical events impinging on existing (and to some extent accidental) social and political structures. Even if there was a historical component, which there could scarcely fail to be in a history of political theory, this was a history like the one envisaged by Petrarch: an elevated conversation of great minds through great texts through the ages, one mountain peak, as it were, responding to another. History was taught as a sequence of positions with later figures responding to difficulties in the positions of their predecessors (whose work they were assumed to know and to whom it was assumed that their own work was really addressed).

Human Nature and History

Bob's first book, *Human Nature and History,* basically argued that liberalism was, for deep-seated reasons inherent in the very logic and structure of its approach, incapable of making up its mind between two incompatible views, neither of which could ever be satisfactory in itself. On the one hand, there was the view that the typical liberal positions were expressions of universal tendencies or aspirations rooted in something like an invariant human nature; since they were part of unchanging human nature, liberal policies could in principle be projected and appropriately applied anywhere at any time. There might be some particular historical conditions that would limit the direct and full realization of liberal principles at some particular time, but these historical restrictions were theoretically unimportant; they were just minor details of the kind that had always to be dealt with when applying fully universal principles to concrete cases. In principle, liberalism itself had validity and could be applied anywhere.

On the other hand, there was the view that liberalism was itself no more than a particular historically contingent, context-dependent response to and intervention in a specific political situation. On this reading its possible relevance to other times, other places, and, as we would say, "other cultures" was an open issue. Liberalism, Bob argued, was condemned eternally to vacillate in a theoretically uncontrolled way between these two, never finding either of them consistently satisfactory (because neither is), and repeatedly failing to give any kind of coherent synthesis of them (because none exists). In a historically very wide-ranging, densely argued and methodologically extremely sophisticated discussion over almost eight hundred pages (in a two-volume work, with almost two thousand footnotes), Bob relentlessly and repeatedly drove home his basic points about the essential incoherence of liberalism as a project, and did so in exhaustive, and sometimes exhausting, detail.

This was not, after all, so far from some of the points that Krigler kept making, although it was expressed in a slightly different way, and Bob not only could deploy the whole panoply of erudition about the ancient world (as indeed Krigler could), but he also added something completely beyond Krigler's ken, namely, a deep familiarity with the details of Anglo-American political thought as it had developed from the seventeenth to the mid-twentieth century. Nevertheless Bob's book suffered from a number of disadvantages. First of all it was a big and very erudite book, and although the writing was clear, it was not really an easy read, being the reflections of a philosophically minded, trained classicist who had spent a decade and a half thinking about J. S. Mill and liberalism. The reader opening the book, and looking for enlightenment about liberalism, was immediately plunged into complex, lengthy, hermeneutic discussions of Cicero, Lactantius, Plutarch, and Polybios, and only after two hundred pages of discussion of the ancients did Hume, Adam Smith, James Mill, Jeremy Bentham, and J. S. Mill appear on the scene. This already made the book rather fall between two stools, because few of those who were interested in Plutarch or Cicero were also interested in J. S. Mill, and most of those interested in J. S. Mill would never have heard of Lactantius or Polybios. Furthermore, although the book makes copious references to contemporary work (that is, books and articles written between the 1920s and the 1960s), Bob made no special attempt to make his discussion relevant to current political events. These features did probably have some effect in preventing the book from having the reception which its intellectual merits and deeper political significance would have warranted.

In contrast to the apparent political abstemiousness of Bob Cumming's work, Robert Paul Wolff's criticism of liberalism was exceedingly acute and savage in the extreme, but it was also robustly activist. He took clear positions on a wide range of political issues of the day. People might have found his positions unpalatable or extreme, but they could be rather clearly located on the existing spectrum of political opinion. His positive commitment to some kind of libertarian socialism shone through everything he said and wrote. He was in a sense playing the game, and even if his way of playing it was not to everyone's taste, this made him a recognizable figure. Sidney, too, although he rarely seemed to be able to settle on any fixed position, simply radiated the joy he felt in the act of collective dialectical investigation. Bob's intelligence, on the other hand, was fastidious and somehow withering in its effect on people and positions. He took apart and demolished the structures of liberalism again and again and again in a highly erudite but completely deadpan way, but also without offering any obvious substitute. The corrosive intention seemed to be universal. No one wanted to hear this, certainly not in 1969; Bob was against liberalism, but also against conservative attempts to appeal simply and directly to human nature, and yet it was hard to place the work next to that of Marcuse (or Malcolm X) as a flaming call to any particular form of action. Although Bob was also a great scholar of Sartre, his work lacked the kind of *actualité* which came easy to contemporary French philosophers. It was as if, to modify slightly Sidney's expression, he was writing for God alone. *Human Nature and History* did get one or two (appropriately) glowing reviews from historians who bothered to read it, but they seemed to be the only ones who did read it. It gathered dust on the shelves of various university libraries, and when the stock at the publisher was exhausted there must not have been any call to reprint it. (It has never, as far as I know, been published in paperback.)

In June 1971 I defended my doctoral dissertation, and prepared to go off to a teaching post in Heidelberg. Since I didn't expect ever to come back to New York, or indeed to the United States, I made an appointment to see Bob Cumming to thank him for all I had learned from him. While killing time before the appointment I saw a copy of Rawls's *Theory of Justice,* which had just been published, in Salters Bookshop, which used to exist on the west side of Broadway between 115th and 116th Streets. I knew from Robert Paul Wolff's lectures more or less what to expect—nothing new, just Rawls adding further elaborate complications to his already rather encumbered theory—but I thought it would not hurt to read it during the summer before the academic year in Heidelberg really began, in October. At the end of my talk with Bob, he noticed that I was carrying the copy of *A Theory of Justice*, and he asked me why I was bothering with that. He seemed to be perfectly *au courant* with it, although it had appeared only a few months previously, but in a way that did not really surprise me very much, because although he didn't go to conferences, he did keep up closely with what one called, coyly in those days, "the literature," and I (naively, no doubt) thought that he, like Sidney, basically read *everything*. He said the same sort of thing I had already heard from Wolff: if you had followed Rawls's previous work, you could see this coming, and it was more-of-same-at-greater-length-and-more-con-volutedly. Rawls, he said, was in the same double bind that all liberals were in—he couldn't decide whether he had a theory of human nature (in his case some version of a Kantian theory of human nature as essentially defined by formal rationality) or a contribution to a particular contingent historical construct. Adding the oddly distorted bits of Kant to the typical liberal mix did not actually clarify anything and certainly did not solve the underlying problem of liberalism. It is hard to see the later history of the development of Rawls's theory as doing anything other than confirming this diagnosis: the early work was more on the model of what Bob had called a human nature view, but when that went down in flames, Rawls shifted over effortlessly to the more historically contextual view which one finds in his later work. Neither one escapes the *aporiai* which Bob diagnosed in his book.

CHAPTER 11

From Heidegger to Adorno

Wir sind nicht hier um Diskurse zu führen

We are not here to conduct discourses.

—Nestroy, *Die schlimmen Buben in der Schule*

I SPENT THE academic year 1967–1968 as a research student in Freiburg im Breisgau. I went there because I wanted, as I have already mentioned, to write something on Heidegger. I hadn't at any distinct point become interested in his work; it was rather that Heidegger, together with Dostoievski, Nietzsche, Freud, Sartre, and (especially) Camus, were simply an integral part of the atmosphere we all breathed in my boarding school. I had a vague idea that I would like to write something on Heidegger and language, but the people I talked to in Freiburg strongly discouraged trying to do this on the grounds that it was really too difficult a topic for a dissertation, and in retrospect I think they were right. In any case I was getting absolutely nowhere thinking about it on my own. In Freiburg I got completely bogged down in working through a set of *Protokolle* of a seminar Heidegger gave on one of the works of Aristotle during the war. I had acquired these by the merest chance in that one of the Greek teachers, Kläre Mylius, who was conducting a seminar I attended on book 4 of Thucydides, had been in Heidegger's seminar during the war and wrote the *Protokoll* for it herself. She lent me a carbon copy.

Insufficient Greek

All the teachers at my school had constantly told me that I didn't know Greek and Latin nearly well enough to do anything serious about ancient literature or culture. I hadn't started Latin until I was twelve and Greek until I was fifteen, and that was just too late, especially since the school could offer only five hours of Latin instruction per week for four years, and the instruction in Greek was a voluntary extra in the final year. One would really need about twice as much instruction as that for about eight or nine years in order to begin to acquire the appropriate competences, and time lost in acquiring the languages in one's early years could never really be made up. The provision in the school, they said, was so meager because of the bizarre requirement by the Pennsylvania Department of Education that we also have chemistry, biology, and physics as part of the curriculum. Math was obviously of central importance, but *chemistry?* Really. In any case, they went on, the cultural context for serious work in classics was missing in the United States. "Look at Jaeger," Krigler said. "Once he left Europe for Harvard, he never did anything serious again. He was reduced to working on *Patristics.*" This was a reference to the fact that after writing his three thick volumes on Greek culture (*Paideia: Die Formung des griechisches Menschen*)[1] while still in Germany, Werner Jaeger had not published much after over a decade at Harvard except a slim volume of lectures entitled *Early Christianity and Greek Paideia.*[2] One had to hear the Heideggerian contempt in Krigler's pronunciation of the word "*Patristics*" fully to appreciate what a come-down it meant in his eyes to end up discussing not Sophokles and Plato, but Gregory of Nyssa.

The advice from my teachers never to expect to be able do anything in classics was partly just the old song "Never praise a boy," but I took it to heart, and devoted my primary attention to other things while trying to maintain only a secondary and amateur interest in the ancient world. Now this decision was coming back to haunt me. I began confusing the deficiencies in my knowledge of Greek—I was taking a seminar on Thucydides and one on Pindar, so I was feeling on especially shaky ground in that regard anyway—with my increasing sense of having lost my footing in reading Heidegger. I began, in fact, to be at a complete loss not only about how one could potentially develop any of Heidegger's views further, but even about how one could coherently comment on them. I began to suspect that Heidegger had in a way been all too successful in achieving one of the goals he had set himself, namely the modernist goal of making his work a completely self-contained universe. He tried to make it impossible to get any external grasp of his views or indulge in any of the usual forms of critical commentary, so that all one could do was either repeat what he said or simply turn one's back on his work. And "repeating Heidegger's views" meant repeating them in his own words, because he held that both everyday language and the traditional language of philosophy were shot through with precisely the kind of philosophical prejudices he was trying to undermine. The dilemma was between either parrot-like repetition or a paraphrase which, precisely by virtue of assimilating his views to more standard positions, made them potentially objects of the usual forms of rational evaluation. Embracing the second horn of the dilemma was a form of begging the question, because Heidegger's thesis was precisely that the terms of any paraphrase would unavoidably contain commitment to at least some of the distorting ontological assumptions which he was trying to reject. This *aporia* seemed paralyzing. The only way out that I could see was to create one's own new hermetic set of terms in order to deal with his writings in a way that did not make one a captive of Heidegger's terminology or of the philosophical tradition. I was not deluded enough to think I was in any position even to undertake that.

I had long taken my inability to understand some things in Heidegger to be simply a deficiency of mine, but the inherently hermetic nature of his project became increasingly clear to me. I then started becoming generally interested in hermetic modes of speech, and began to read Paul Celan seriously. My attempts to do this acquired a certain extra impetus because while I was there, Celan gave a reading in Freiburg. In fact, he came to the city, it seems, partly to talk to Heidegger, and he later published a poem ("Todtnauberg") about their meeting.[3] Much of Celan's later work had not, of course, even been written in 1967–1968, but *Von Schwelle zu Schwelle* and *Mohn und Gedächtnis* were available, as was the fascinating *Der Meridian*.[4]

Paul Celan

The anarcho-communist sensibility of Celan's early body of work expressed itself in poems which contained strings of "dark" images— "dark" (*dunkel*) meaning in the first instance "not illuminated," "obscure," "difficult to make out," but then perhaps also "gloomy," "cheerless."[5] The obscurity was partly a matter of unusual syntax and lexis in the imagery itself. So in the last poem of *Von Schwelle zu Schwelle*, one reads about some people who are rowing "*dem Einbaum waldher vermählt / von Himmeln umgeiert die Arme.*" This means something like "from the forest (*waldher*) married to the canoe-made-of-

the-hollowed-out-trunk-of-a-single-tree (*Einbaum*)/their arms vultured-around by skies."[6] The adverb *waldher* and the verb *umgeiern*
are semantically transparent in themselves, but they are not exactly
part of everyday diction, and putting them together with the rest of
the phrase yields a colossally complex and certainly not immediately
comprehensible unit. Partly the obscurity was about the connection
between different parts of the poem. Thus my favorite poem in the
collection *Shibboleth* is full of references to the Spanish Civil War
(Madrid, *no pasarán*), but the last strophe reads:

> *Einhorn:*
> *du weißt um die Steine*
> *du weißt um das Wasser*
> *komm*
> *ich führe dich hinweg*
> *zu den Stimmen*
> *von Estremadura.*

> Unicorn:/you know about the stones/you know about the
> water/come/I'll lead you away/to the voices/of Estremadura

Estremadura is not out of place in a poem which seems partly to
be about Spain, and the stones and the water occur very frequently
in Celan's poems, but what about the unicorn and why should it be
taken to the voices of Estremadura? I couldn't prevent myself from
associating the unicorn with the canoe made from hollowing out the
trunk of a single tree (*Einhorn/Einbaum*), but I strongly suspected
that that was just an idiosyncrasy of mine.[7] The poems were extremely
lovely, but they required a distinct effort of inhibiting an impulse to
ask for a certain kind of clarity. The absence of that kind of clarity
was not a failure or a bit of individual willfulness on the part of the

poet. Rather Celan held that readers should not only accept, they should actively expect authors to force them to stretch themselves, and to offer them things that were really out of their reach: "*Ne nous rapprochez le manque de clarté puisque nous en faisons profession*" (Do not reproach us for lack of clarity: that is something we aspire to).[8] The reason for this "profession" on the part of the poet has something to do with what Celan calls the "majesty of the absurd,"[9] which, in turn, is part of what makes us human and allows us to be humane. Celan's, one might say, is the true atheism: the basic fact about the universe is that it is infinitely pointless, utterly lacking in any kind of meaning. It is not just that people die or that sometimes human projects are futile and pointless, but that mortality and futility are *infinite*. Poetry expresses this fact. As he puts it: "*Die Dichtung, meine Damen und Herren, diese Unendlichsprechung von lauter Sterblichkeit und Umsonst,*" that is, "Poetry, ladies and gentlemen, that way of declaring that nothing-but-mortality and futility/pointlessness/for-nothingness are infinite."[10] Yet against this general background occasionally humans can encounter each other, can experience humane contact and even a certain limited understanding. How this happens is completely mysterious (Celan speaks of the "*Geheimnis der Begegnung*"[11]), and in such an encounter the humans involved will never become totally transparent to each other (or, presumably, to themselves). The poem tries to be the locus at which such a humane encounter can occur.[12] The humane is always in some sense congenitally unclear.[13]

Actually Celan distinguishes two obscurities in modern poetry.[14] One is the "congenital" darkness of anything which concerns humans and their encounters (with others or with themselves), and the second concerns a specific tendency to obscurity which arises from poetic language, especially in the modern world. Contemporary poetic speech tends to extreme ellipsis and condensed expression, even to the extent of falling silent completely (*"eine starke Neigung zum Verstummen"*[15]). I wish to suggest a distinction of a different sort between two different historical constellations, both of which gave prominence to the obscure. The obscurity in each case is of a different kind. First, there is a hierophantic obscurity, that is, a kind of sacerdotal darkness of expression associated with a certain kind of social exclusion.[16] Only the high priest or the *vates* is really in the know, has access to something special, which, in addition, he cannot express clearly to those who are not already initiated into the appropriate secrets. Often this is associated with a rank-ordering within the group, which is taken to reflect degrees of closeness to (insight into) the truth. In cases that fall under this category, ever greater obscurity of expression (toward those of the common populace, the uninitiated) is the external concomitant to deeper and deeper insight. The circle around the poet Stefan George was a good instance of this kind of socially organized and managed obscurity.[17] In some cases, the management in fact amounted to an active generation of artificial obscurities, that is, to mystification. In philosophy, Hans-Georg Gadamer, who was not a direct associate of George's circle, had his own, rather similar, project.[18] It is important to see that Celan's obscurity is of a completely different kind from this socially exclusionary esotericism. It is demotic, not hierophantic. Obscurity is the universal fate of all human interactions. Failure of comprehension—the missed meeting[19]—is in fact the usual human state, but it results from the inherent difficulties of all human situations, from human weakness, from our inability or refusal to understand; but none of these is the same thing as exclusion, and there can be no hierarchy because no one has any special standing vis-à-vis any truth, in fact not even vis-à-vis his or her own experience.[20] Celan was not a priest of any kind—high or low—and did not want to be one, and he had friends but no "circle."

Kretzschmar

It was in this context that I started reading Adorno. I knew something about him second-hand from a seminar I had taken, in 1964, on Thomas Mann, in which we had read *Doktor Faustus*. The instructor, Theodore Ziolkowski, had talked about Adorno and Mann in exile in Southern California during the Second World War and about the way in which the musical analyses which Mann attributes to the character Kretzschmar in the book were really taken from discussions he had had with Adorno. Mann had even written a small book about the genesis of the novel (*Die Entstehung des "Doktor Faustus"*), which Ziolkowski encouraged us to read.[21] I didn't have time to do that in 1964, but in 1967 when I was sitting in the *Seminarbibliothek* in one of the seminars in Freiburg, I was getting nowhere with whatever text I was reading and stood up to stretch my legs. I wandered around and found Adorno's *Prismen* on the shelf.[22] I was so taken by it that I began to read other works by Adorno more systematically, starting with *Negative Dialektik*.[23]

Several things made an immediate impression on me. One was the claim that philosophy could not be summarized (*referiert*). It was, at any rate, not directed at producing detachable propositions or theses that could be extracted and taken away from the whole of the text at the end. To think about philosophy in this way was to miss the point that philosophical claims were always embedded and had their meaning in a specific context of reflection. The reflective process itself was what one needed to keep one's eye on. Obviously, I thought, this did not mean that one could never say anything about what a philosopher was getting at, or draw conclusions from it for action; this was the opposite mistake—to misunderstand it like that would be to make the same kind of error that Adorno was trying to diagnose.

Adorno went on to claim that the extreme demand that conclusions must be able to be stated in the form of a simple set of "results" could itself be a form of social oppression. Discussion in the public domain was very frequently stacked against those who held minority, deviant, or merely novel views, and those who insisted on having a clear and simple "result" often wanted to extract something that they could use against you in a game that was rigged anyway. In a way Adorno's view was no different from some of the things that one could find in Heidegger, who, after all, kept talking about the "path" of thinking, as if the travel itself was more important than the destination, and about the way in which ordinary language distorted thought. Nevertheless, Heidegger tended to treat at least other philosophers as if their work could be precisely summed up, infinitely ruminating on individual sentences by Parmenides or Anaximander. This had made it impossible for me to see this point about summaries, results, and conclusions expressed in Heidegger's work.

The second impressive thing about Adorno was his general agreement with Celan on the issue of clarity: easy comprehensibility was not an invariably positive feature of discourse. Adorno, however, gave a less existential and more sociologically and politically nuanced account of the reasons for being suspicious of clarity. Everyday language is corrupt because of its integration into the existing political and economic system, and, as such, it is itself part of an apparatus of repression. Requiring that any thought be expressed in an easily comprehensible way is a repressive demand. It *sounds* very democratic and anti-elitist to demand that authors, for instance, express themselves in ways that can easily and immediately be understood by everyone, but only if you fail to realize that what counts as clear and comprehensible is to a significant extent limited to what is thought to be compatible with the status quo. "Make it easy for everyone to understand" is a way of filtering out and excluding radical suggestions that might represent genuine alternatives to the present. Lack of complete clarity can be unavoidable, if it characterizes the expression of a real possibility that is so novel it doesn't really fit into available categories. This might be another reason to look favorably on *lectio difficilior.*

Unclarity

Because this point is particularly important and has also not, it seems to me, been really assimilated and internalized especially by some contemporary philosophers, I will expatiate on it.

In his lectures, Robert Paul Wolff reported a conversation he had had with Herbert Marcuse. Marcuse had written his *Habilitationsschrift*— a kind of second doctoral dissertation—on Hegel under the supervision of Heidegger, and when Wolff made a disobliging remark to the effect that Hegel's writings were very "unclear," Marcuse got exercised and began to speak with great insistency. When this happened, though, his thick German accent made him difficult to understand. Wolff understood him to be shouting "Hm, clarity is a virtue; Hm, clarity is a virtue," and hastened to agree with him that clarity was one of the most important philosophical virtues, but every time Wolff expressed what he thought was agreement, Marcuse got more upset and became more difficult to understand. Only gradually did it dawn on Wolff that what he had taken to be throat-clearing at the beginning of a sentence ("Hm") was Marcuse's phonetic rendering of the English syllable "un-," so Marcuse had been shouting, "Unclarity is a virtue; unclarity is a virtue."

A person's immediate reaction to a statement like "Unclarity can be a virtue" is a criterion by which one can distinguish two kinds of minds. For some, for instance, followers—perhaps at a great distance—of Descartes, the very idea that unclarity could have any value is anathema. The only possible reason a statement might not be clear is that the speaker is not being careful, is confused, or is consciously being evasive, manipulative, or deceitful. Anyone who doesn't stand up for the indispensable paramountcy of the virtue of clarity is an obscurantist, an enemy of science and of the Enlightenment, perhaps even a proto-fascist. For others, any set of assertions that contain something genuinely new and original is very likely indeed—at least at first—to fail to count as being completely clear. Partly this may be because genuinely novel suggestions won't yet be fully worked out, but a more significant reason is that they will violate conventional expectations and thought patterns and also will not be firmly integrated into existing routinized practices and norms.

One must initially resist a certain form of bullying from the side of the Cartesians, who will have a tendency to assume that the distinction between "clear" and "unclear" is itself not in need of analysis and explication. Reading the later work of the philosopher Ludwig Wittgenstein, however, convinced many people that "meaning" was inherently and not merely accidently connected to patterns of social action, and if that is the case, then the same will be true of "clarity."[24] Think of trying to explain conic sections to a member of an indigenous group in the Amazon in their language, or of trying to make it clear to them what an antibiotic is and how it works. Or think of giving a clear account of the electoral system of some large parliamentary democracy to Ancient Egyptian priests, or of the Highway Code to inhabitants of the tundra. In these cases the social institutions, routines, habits of behavior, and regular patterns of action—the laboratories, medical practices, highway signs, polling places, synods and councils—that would give substance to the idea of a "clear account" are simply lacking.

Wolff had been nonplussed by Marcuse's remark, I take it, because he took "Unclarity is a virtue" to be something like one of Descartes's "rules for the direction of the mind," that is, as a recommendation for individual action: "aspire to unclarity." This does indeed not seem to be especially good advice in most situations. However, a little reflection should suffice to see that this was based on a misapprehension. Marcuse's comment is most plausibly understood as a remark about what turns out to be true (or to have been true) about human society and history, and it is a comment made from an irreducibly third-person perspective. It can frequently turn out to have been a good thing to have violated a given, imposed system of categories, which purportedly defined clear thinking. If "clarity/unclarity" is not a distinction fixed in the nature of reality itself, but a function of our linguistic and social habits, institutions, modes of acting, and preconceptions, which could always be different from what they are, then failure to fit smoothly into those existing categories at least always has the advantage of drawing our attention to the constructed nature of the distinction. Whether or not this virtue will outweigh the inconveniencies associated with it, is something that one would have to decide in the particular case in question. The beginning of understanding in this area is *not* to adopt the liberal assumption that the *only* possible context for meaning is to be found in the content of the consciousness of the sovereign individual (in one or another of its concrete or idealized forms, for instance the Kantian form).[25]

"Clear" is always a term used in a context. It always means "clear enough," but clear enough for what purpose, and how much is enough? So to hold that there is some kind of absolute clarity, you must subscribe to one or another of two further doctrines, neither of which is especially plausible. One of these is to be convinced of the unsurpassable moral and political health and virtue of your own momentary social practices and institutions and the forms of speech and of common sense embedded in them. You must assume, for instance, that history has come to an end with us and we have (basically) the final, the ideally right social formation. The alternative is to believe that humans have preternaturally strong powers of abstraction, detachment, imagination, and formalization, and that by dint of exercising this capacity we can create a freestanding realm of meaning which is fully functional but not connected at all to human action and human history.[26]

Negativity

The final thing I found in Adorno's texts which attracted my attention was a fully unabashed defense of negativity. Not only could the demand for a "clear result" be a form of repression, but the same could be true of the relentless requirement that a critic present "something positive" or a "positive alternative" to the state of affairs being criticized. It was part of a strategy for the defense of the status quo. To insist that anyone who criticized existing conditions must have a clear, easily formulable proposal for something to replace it, was to impose on the critic an inappropriately severe demand. In the reception (or rather non-reception) of Bob's work I thought I saw something like this at work. It was almost as if it was in some way *his* fault, not that of J. S. Mill, that Mill's views were so pathetically inadequate. I filed this part of Adorno away in the same mental drawer that contained Marcuse's *Repressive Toleranz*.

Finally, I read Adorno's *Minima moralia*, which is, among other things, an extended criticism of some of the central tenets of liberalism. The subject isn't naturally sovereign, but rather is something which, because it is essentially constituted by social relations, can attain only the partial and minimal autonomy of which it is capable by virtue of becoming aware of that dependency. Furthermore, the liberal overvalues both clarity and free discussion. This, Adorno claims in *Minima moralia*, is completely wrong. The idea that truth is simple and can be easily formulated, and made accessible to all if only, for instance, free discussion is permitted, is a complete error. Adorno is particularly scathing about what he calls the "liberal fiction" that truth is universally communicable.[27] My reading of Celan freed me from any inclination to assume—as many contemporary philosophers insinuate one should—that obscurity must be either a matter of individual deficiency—a failure to be as clear as one could be—or of intentional obfuscation.

In addition, my religion classes with Krigler had already made me familiar with suspicion of the idea that free discussion is a panacea. Krigler pointed out that any theoretical difficulties that arose about the idea of "free discussion" were bound also immediately to infect the associated notion of "consensus." "Consensus" of a kind (the *consensus omnium fidelium*—consensus of all the faithful[28]) was one component of the traditional Catholic set of sources of recognized guidance (see Chapter 4), but it was only one component. It was an infelicitous novelty for certain partisans of the papacy to try to extract "papal authority" out of the complex historical fabric of Catholic belief and practice—to isolate, purify, intensify, and, in fact, absolutize it, just as it had been an unfortunate misunderstanding of history, religion, and hermeneutics for the Protestant fundamentalists to try to absolutize "Scripture" as they had done. Equally, though, one could not treat any form of consensus as an utterly infallible guide to belief and action. If Krigler had been able to foresee later developments in philosophy, I am sure he would have made a point of specifically rejecting the claim that any kind of hypothetical, counterfactual, implied, idealized, or anticipatory consensus could form the Archimedean point of a normative theory.

Just as my experience in reading the writings of Robert Paul Wolff and listening to his lectures had inoculated me against Rawls, and Bob Cumming's book had the same effect for J. S. Mill, so reading Adorno in Freiburg in 1967–1968 made it impossible for me to accept even slightly deviant forms of liberalism like that proposed in numerous works by Habermas, who abandons the traditional concept of the sovereign subject, but still bases his view on some particularly naive ideas about idealized free discussion and on a baroque theory of "consensus."

CHAPTER 12

Past, Present, Future

Sollen sich trösten! Alles geht vorüber, in hundert Jahren sind ganz andere Buben auf der Welt.

Don't be concerned. Everything passes away, in a hundred years there will be completely different boys in the world.

—Nestroy, *Die schlimmen Buben in der Schule*

JUST A FEW YEARS after I graduated from my secondary school, it began to undergo a radical change. The Hungarian and Spanish priests who had formed the staff gradually came to be replaced by US-born staff, and the boarding section of the school closed when the reservoir of recently arrived Hungarian refugee boys dried up. The region around the school was sufficiently close to Philadelphia for it to begin to become increasingly suburbanized, and this had consequences for the pool of pupils available for what had become fully a day school. This was an inevitable part of the process by which this essentially foreign body was assimilated into the larger society of which it was a part. I believe some of the more intrepid members of the order moved to Appalachia and founded a school there in order to pursue their vocation of the education of the poor.

The bubble of artificially trapped air from 1930s Budapest in any case finally burst.

Nothing that has happened in the fifty years since I finished my doctoral dissertation in 1971 has really had a radical effect in shaking the basic way of viewing the world which I had acquired at my boarding school and at university, and which has been in place since then. I have learned a lot since I first sat in Krigler's religion class in autumn 1959, but, although in the years thereafter I did form new opinions on lots of particular topics to which I had previously given no thought, changed my mind on lots of individual issues, got to know several charismatic and highly intelligent people and even modified some of my attitudes in various ways, one thing that was already fixed and remained so for the next fifty years was my underlying assumption that the tradition which runs from Locke, through J. S. Mill, to Rawls was not the place to look for insight into anything. I mentioned that my school was a very highly developed instance of a total institution, and so one might ask the question now whether I had not simply been very effectively and lastingly brainwashed there. One might also wonder whether the fact that I have changed so few of my basic attitudes over time is not an expression of some kind of defect in my character or life, a failure to be attentive to the world around me, indolence, lack of imagination, willful perversity, or just obtuseness. I don't myself feel that this is the case. After all, to start with, my Catholic education failed in its most fundamental task of making me a good (or, for that matter, even a bad) Catholic. So I was clearly not just a blank sheet of paper waiting to take whatever impress the order wished to impose on it.

I see the last fifty years as a period during which a lot of the chaff that I picked up from various sources was winnowed away by my own reflection, my experience, and the force of external events, leaving a core of views, approaches, and attitudes that have survived, and by virtue of that have in a sense stood the test of time. I failed, in other words, to acquire the positive worldview that I was supposed to (Catholicism), but I did acquire a deep, abiding, and, as the years went on, increasingly reflective aversion to certain concepts, theories, arguments, ways of seeing the world, and forms of sensibility. Such aversions can, in my view, be of great importance and are by no means necessarily irrational. In his last and unfinished book, *Ästhetische Theorie*, Adorno talks about the way in which a "canon of prohibitions" can get established as a central part of certain modern aesthetic movements.[1] Artists felt, for one reason or another, that they could not permit themselves anymore to write, paint, or compose "like *that*"— that is, as some of their predecessors and contemporaries had written, painted, or composed: writing or composing "like *that*" was kitschy, maudlin, passé, banal, or what have you. Thus, at certain points in their careers, members of the Second Viennese School of composers would not have used major triads in their works because they thought that these musical figures had been overused and were expressively "exhausted" (*verbraucht*). Brecht had a similar experience in 1938, when he wrote,

> *In meinem Lied ein Reim*
> *käme mir fast vor wie Übermut*
>
> A rhyme in my song
> would seem to me almost
> presumptuous.[2]

A "canon of prohibitions" can in principle change over time, but that is a separate issue. In my own case, I have seen no reason for fundamental modification of mine.

Human social and political life, of course, is not exactly the same thing as artistic activity, and different elements will play a role in motivating systematic avoidance in music or literature and in politics. Still, there can be important similarities. The accidents of history opened a brief window of time in a particular place in which I was enabled to develop a rudimentary canon of aversions in politics, ethics, and philosophy, which in turn permitted me at least partially to avoid becoming a liberal. Why partially, though? The reason is that societies are overwhelming structures, and in my case there was no way completely to escape participation in interlocking and mutually reinforcing social institutions that were structured so as to embody "liberal" conceptions. Certainly the vocabulary of "liberalism" is the dominant and virtually all-pervasive idiom of our thought and speech, and I cannot claim to be completely uninfluenced by that. Its terminology and conceptions inform even the everyday language we use. This means that a person like me must be constantly bi-ocular and bi-lingual.[3] I use in everyday life terms which I know have associations I deeply deplore or reject, but I am unable, if I am to avoid constant and pointless pedantry or complete incomprehension, to use any other with the fluency and immediate self-evidence that easy everyday communication requires. So, although I am an atheist, I find myself saying things like "If that happens, then God help us all" without thinking that this commits me even to a belief in the existence of gods, much less to a particular theology in which the purported god(s) was/were sufficiently interested in the affairs of humanity for it to make sense to invoke his, her, their, or its help. I even blithely use a system of dates calculated from the notional year in which "Our Lord, Jesus Christ" was born, and employ the abbreviation AD (*anno Domini*, "in the year of the Lord") without thinking that this implies that I have accepted Jesus as my Lord. Equally, I find the whole apparatus of "rights" as usually deployed conceptually completely misguided. I have a number of different reasons for holding this view, one of which is the close association of our usual conception of "rights" with the notion of the sovereign individual subject, who is proposed as the bearer of such rights.[4] Nevertheless, in everyday life I feel no compunction about using the word "rights" to make myself understood to others.

There is nothing inherently wrong with failure to be particularly reflective, just using the existing available language as everyone else does, and not in general tying oneself in knots or turning somersaults to make one's speech conform to some ideal of correctness. We may have an obligation to avoid offensive speech, but we don't have an obligation either to eloquence or to exactness of expression or even to exceptional thoughtfulness. Many people, even people who pursue philosophy as a profession, are greatly at ease in one or another of the more comfortable niches which our world provides for those with certain saleable skills, like those of argumentation, skills that can be practiced without distancing oneself too much from the assumptions embedded in the local social practices. Still, one might think that this kind of taking one's distance should be part of any attempt to continue in the tradition that goes back to Sokrates. Continuing to develop that tradition would imply also cultivating bi-ocular vision. Although philosophers cannot pretend to be the voice of universal reason or propose an all-encompassing worldview, they should try to remain committed to abstracting as much as possible from the particular context in which they find themselves. Thus, they should be very wary of becoming too comfortable with the particular society, or the particular niche within society, which they happen to inhabit. This remains true despite the fact that complete abstraction is impossible and a "view from nowhere" does not exist.

The forces of alterity may have no alternative if they are to survive the glacial impact of liberalism but to take very peculiar forms indeed. I have tried in this book to describe one of these xenomorphs— the outlandish forms—which these alternatives may take by telling a real story, in fact (part of) my story. It was possible to have opinions and attitudes different from those prescribed by liberalism. What my story shows perhaps is how off-beat and unusual the circumstances had to be for this to be possible—a total institution like a benevolent version of one of the castles in a novel by the Marquis de Sade, run by and for Hungarian refugees, effectively detached from its surrounding space and time. There are actually lots of alternatives to liberalism, but in my case the relevant one was Catholicism of this peculiar but nonauthoritarian kind. Although I failed to embrace it, exposure to it in the very early 1960s had served me well in allowing me to avoid some intellectual, moral, and political dead ends, and to pass through and survive various temporary illusions. In 1971, then, all that remained for me to do was to rid myself of some fragments of Kantianism that had managed to insinuate themselves into my mind during my time at university, probably as a result of the overwhelming, if half unconscious, bias in that direction which structures the dominant form of academic instruction. That took me about twenty years.

Liberalism in Our World

It is hard to see how the traditional remedies of liberalism will be of any help in the world we now inhabit. My teachers at school and university held that liberalism was wrong-headed and that many of its central doctrines were simply false. That was a theoretical judgment which still seems to me to be true. However, in addition, liberalism has begun to show itself in an increasingly unmistakable way to be at best irrelevant and at worst actively deleterious to human well-being. We live in a society in which we are under universal uninterrupted electronic surveillance which allows continuous tracking of virtually all our movements, but also all our opinions and our desires to the extent to which they leave any visible trace in the world at all, and which makes the dystopian vision of *1984* look crude and underdeveloped by comparison. What is more, no one really wants to go back to the days before Amazon, Google, CCTV cameras in public spaces, computer analysis of "big data" sets, and the internet. I would myself be pleased to return to the mechanical typewriter and the corner public telephone, but I am under no illusion about the fact that for anyone under the age of fifty there is no conceivable alternative to universal electronic connection. In fact most people don't want to leave this universe or abolish it. So where exactly in it could the sovereign individual chooser, surrounded by a protected private sphere, be located? Who will provide this protection? Who will control the protectors? Do we need a global agency to oversee the collection and use of data? Is the creation of such an agency part of a liberal agenda? Is liberalism committed to the lightest possible regulatory touch on the financial services industry and the respect for all existing forms of ownership and entitlement? The financial crisis of 2008 was a direct effect of the application of liberal doctrines to the banking system. The only remedies liberals seem to have in their medicine chest to prevent a recurrence of such a crisis seem toothless almost to the point of absurdity.

Is further discussion "under ideal conditions" going to make all the participants eventually see each others' points of view and agree on some compromise? How well has discussion worked in getting the banks under control up to now? Will further discussion of Brexit in the UK be helpful? Should we continue to discuss whether the

COVID virus and the pandemic really exist? Or whether Trump really won the 2020 US presidential election? Or whether there really is, as some adherents of QAnon assert, a conspiracy of diabolic pedophiles who are pulling strings behind the scenes and dominating public discourse and politics in the West? Where exactly is the point of neutrality on which we can all agree and from which we can adjudicate these claims?

Our species is now committing suicide by destroying our natural environment. It seems impossible to imagine how catastrophe could be avoided without significant coercive measures directed against the major actors and institutions of our current economic system.[5] "Liberalism," in the sense in which I have been using the term in this book, is committed to the inviolability of individual taste and opinion, the need to protect maximum unfettered individual choice, and free enterprise. Anyone who, in our world, can see a viable path from this conception to a situation in which we avoid ecological disaster has much sharper vision than mine.

Vision, Hope, and Action

Where does that leave someone like me now? I have already mentioned that in this book I am engaged in narration, not argumentation. I am not, that is, trying to refute liberalism, but to tell the story of the course of a human life. I will be very pleased if readers of this text come, as a result of reading it, to change some of their own views and attitudes, but I realize that that is largely out of my control.

I have also mentioned two of the aspects of Adorno's philosophy which it seemed to me important to assimilate: the idea that philosophy is not essentially about stating detachable conclusions and the idea that there is nothing wrong with negativity. Philosophy is essentially a matter of criticism, of constant evaluative activity. One objection that is often raised against this is that no view like this could ever be a proper philosophical guide to action, and perhaps that is in some sense right. Is it, however, obvious that one could and should have a philosophical guide to action? If philosophy is a form of potentially continuous mental and spiritual activity, perhaps it is a mistake from the very start to expect it to provide us, as it were from its own resources, with principles or goals and a motivation to act on them. Perhaps the real false step historically was from Sokrates, who said he knew nothing and spent his whole life assessing claims, to the dogmatism of Plato.

A further worry might be that the bi-ocular vision which I proposed earlier, or the lack of an explicit worldview or of some systematic kind of overarching hope for human improvement, might make commitment or action impossible. I don't see why any of this should be the case. Even without hope, we still can, and should, act.[6] The orchestra of the *Titanic* is said to have continued to play until the musicians fell into the sea. Did they (falsely) hope the ship would eventually right itself on its own? Did they *all* have religious belief in some transcendental salvation? Were they motivated by the thought that in playing they were doing something for those others still alive? Is it inconceivable that they would continue to play even if they were the last ones alive (and they knew it)? Sometimes in recent philosophic discussion this kind of action is subsumed under the category of "action from an identity": that is, we are doing this, not because we think it will lead to anything at all, but because we are persons of this kind, or we wish to be persons of this kind. We are musicians and will stay true to that profession independently of whether or not there is any hope that doing what we do will have any particular consequences. Krigler used to say that if you did what you thought you ought to, even though you could see no meaning in the universe at all and you thought your own action was totally pointless, you were exhibiting a very advanced kind of religious sensibility.

In a more secular idiom, I have always taken the aphorism by René Char which I cited at the start of this book—*Ne t'attarde pas à l'ornière des resultats* (Don't dawdle in the rut of results)—as an injunction to disconnect action from dependency on results. To the extent to which this is possible, action without hope is, too. Char was perfectly capable of calculating future effects, and acting on those calculations. Aphorism 138 of *Les Feuillets d'Hypnos* describes the horrifying day on which he watched the execution of a friend from a small hill just outside the village where he was hiding.[7] He had a machine pistol and as many men with him as the group of SS soldiers who were conducting the execution. He did not fire "because *at any cost* that village had to be spared" (*parce que ce village devrait être épargné* à tout prix) from the inevitable reprisals the SS would have launched if some of its soldiers had been killed in the village.

People can lose their motivation to act for all kinds of peculiar reasons, and it is perfectly possible that people who convince themselves that the pointlessness of an action is a reason to abstain from it will not be motivated to perform it, but that is because of what they have persuaded themselves to believe about action. It is by no means necessary to adopt this demotivating attitude.

We have, I think, no choice but to act because of the people we are. Foucault at one point distinguishes between the "ethos of the Enlightenment" and the "doctrines of the Enlightenment."[8] The former designates a set of dispositions and habits of mind and action which are centered around investigating the world around us, reflecting on experience, and questioning the beliefs people hold and the claims they make (including those I myself make), and, if necessary, criticizing them. The latter comprises a set of assumptions about science, progress, human psychology, the nature and goals of human society, and so forth. Foucault thinks that we can and should cleave to the first without necessarily endorsing the second. It is not that the activity of critical reflection can take place in a vacuum or in a situation of entire and complete flux of opinion and belief. Of course, at any one time certain beliefs will have utterly discredited themselves either epistemically or morally, and others will not *at that time* seem equally compromised. We start from cognitive positions that we have acquired in complicated ways, ways in which an element of chance plays an important role, but then we can sometimes go on from there and criticize our beliefs and habits in the hope of improving them. From the fact that we can sometimes clearly improve them, it does not follow that there is any invariable concept of "criticism," "truth," or even "improvement" which we can extract theoretically from the flux and present in a pristine conceptual form. Our situation could change and certainly will eventually change, but at the moment we have good reason to cultivate criticism, and to the extent to which philosophy enacts itself as criticism of this type, we now have reason to continue the practice. It is also the case that the history of philosophy can be treated as part of the large imaginative reservoir of diverse ways of thinking and acting to which literate humans have access, and some of the analyses and proposals historical philosophers have offered might continue to be of interest to us. Having such a resource is a great advantage to humans. In the end, though, we need to decide what sort of people we wish to be as individuals and also, collectively, as group agents. Philosophy can have a role in this, but we should also draw on much wider resources than philosophy itself can provide.

notes

Abbreviations

KSA   *Friedrich Nietzsche: Kritische Studienausgabe,*
15 vols., ed. Giorgio Colli and Mazzino
Montinari (de Gruyter, 1967–1988).

MEW   *Marx-Engels-Werke,* 44 vols. (Dietz, 1968).

MM   Theodor Wiesengrund Adorno, *Minima
moralia* (Suhrkamp, 1951), cited by
§-number.

PCM   Paul Celan, *Der Meridian und andere Prosa*
(Suhrkamp, 1968).

Preface

1. MEW Erg. 1, 536.

Introduction

1. See my *History and Illusion in Politics* (Cambridge University Press,
1999).

2. John Dunn has shown the great relevance of historical reflection on the changing meaning of the term "democracy" in his *Setting the People Free: The Story of Democracy* (Atlantic, 2005).

3. KSA 5, 316–318.

4. See Hartmut Leppin, *Die frühen Christen: Von den Anfängen bis Konstantin* (Beck, 2018), which gives numerous instances of this kind of thing.

5. Thomas Kuhn, *The Structure of Scientific Revolutions* (University of Chicago Press, 1962) and Imre Lakatos and Alan Musgrave, eds., *Criticism and the Growth of Knowledge* (1965; Cambridge University Press, 2018).

6. MEW 1, 347–391.

7. MM §151.

8. *Dissoi logoi* is the name modern scholars give to an ancient text from about the time of Sokrates and Plato in which parallel arguments are presented for and against such propositions as that the good and the bad are identical with one another. See Hermann Diels and Walter Kranz, *Fragmente der Vorsokratiker* (Weidmannsche Verlagsbuchhandlung, 1951), vol. 2, 405–416.

9. Robert Nozick, *Philosophical Explanations* (Harvard University Press, 1981), preface. One can find a pale, but for me still unpalatable, reflection of this in Habermas's use of the formula "*der eigentümlich zwanglose Zwang des besseren Arguments*": see Jürgen Habermas, *Theorie des kommunikativen Handelns* (Suhrkamp, 1981).

chapter 1 My Fate

1. See Raymond Geuss, "*Die Hoffnung*," in Sarah Bianchi, ed., *Auf Nietzsches Balkon III: Beiträge aus der Villa Silberblick* (Bauhaus-Universitätsverlag, 2018), 233–236.

2. Johann Wolfgang von Goethe, "Beginning of March 1832," *Gespräche mit Eckermann in den letzten Jahren seines Lebens* (Tempel-Verlag, n.d.), vol. 2, 73ff. In the late poem *Urworte. Orphisch* (in his *Gedichte*, ed. Heinz Nicolai [Insel, 1982], 879), Goethe gives a stylized description of a typical human life as moving through a series of distinct stages, each described by a Greek term: Daimon, Tyche, Eros, Ananke, Elpis. The fact that a positively evaluated Elpis comes last in this sequence, after

Ananke, is a clear indication that Goethe, despite his professed pagan polytheism, was actually an optimistic post-Christian poet.

3. René Char, *Oeuvres complètes,* Pléiade (Gallimard, 1983), 175.
4. The other version of the story he told was that he had been sent home because he "was too inflexible to be a Catholic priest," which says more about him—he did have a tendency to high moral dudgeon in some areas—than about the demands of the priesthood.
5. Erwin Goffmann, *Asylums: Essays on the Social Situation of Mental Patients and Other Inmates* (Anchor, 1961).

chapter 2 **Liberalism**

1. See my *Public Goods, Private Goods* (Princeton University Press, 2001).
2. Another kind of paper that Sidney encouraged people to avoid writing was "the flea." If you have a flea it itches terribly, but no one else much cares. Then there was "the ghoul," which disinters old positions everyone had forgotten about in order merely once again to dismember and destroy them savagely and then rebury them with great fanfare.
3. "*Menj a víz alá*" (Go drown yourself) was a frequently used imprecation—*very* mild and unimaginative by prevailing Hungarian standards—which I heard almost every day. Andras's father had thrown himself onto the underground (subway) track at 96th Street station in New York while still in exile. For a while, I think, Hungary had a per capita suicide rate that almost rivaled that of Japan.
4. See my *Who Needs a World View?* (Harvard University Press, 2020), 3–12.
5. "There is no salvation outside the church," although the absence of articles in Latin makes it possible to read this as "Outside a church [that is, some church or other] there is no salvation."
6. Thomas Carlyle, ed., *Oliver Cromwell's Letters and Speeches* (Chapman and Hall, 1869), vol. 2, 217.
7. The writings by Michel Foucault which have made this view now a commonplace were not even written in 1960 when Krigler was saying this kind of thing.
8. See especially Bernhard Dombart and Alfons Kalb, eds., *Augustini de civ. dei* (Teubner, 1981), book 5.
9. MM §29.

chapter 3 **Authoritarianism**

1. That is why an extermination camp is not really a very good place to look if one wishes to understand authority or authoritarianism. In *If This Is a Man* (Abacus, 1991), Primo Levi reports that when he asked a guard in Auschwitz why a certain regulation was in force, the guard replied: "*Hier ist kein Warum*" (Here there is no Why). This indicates an attempt to institute a complete rupture between action, the existing network of mutual human expectations, and ratiocination. As such, it represents not so much the *non plus ultra* of authoritarianism, as an attempt to move beyond authority altogether and into the realm of pure thuggery. In a way, in giving Levi this answer, the guard was performing a pragmatic contradiction. If there really was *no* "why" in the camp, the guard should not have answered Levi at all: in doing so he was explaining that explanations did not exist. The fact that the guard was contradicting himself was little consolation to Levi, much less to the others who were forced into the gas chambers without even this minimal verbal interaction. This ought not to make us imagine we can get any particular ethical or political traction out of pointing out contradictions like this. All it shows is that it is best not to focus on examples like this, if one wishes to understand claims about "authority."

2. Max Weber, *Wirtschaft und Gesellschaft* (Mohr, 1972), 140–148, 650–688.

3. I had direct experience of this in the mid-1970s, when one of my cousins who was a policeman in Philadelphia decided that he wished to move to New York. He asked me to inquire about employment in the New York City Police Department. At that time I had shoulder-length hair and my general appearance was both unathletic and informal. The faces of the cops in the precinct office as I explained to them that I wanted an application form to join the NYPD indicated to me that they had a clear conception, to which I did not conform, of the appearance which a policeman should have in order to project a sense of natural authority.

4. The great Roman historian Theodor Mommsen said that "*auctoritas*" was an inherently "fuzzy" concept (*verschwommen*) and that it "resisted strict definition" (*ein sich aller strengen Definition entziehendes Wort*): Theodor Mommsen, *Römisches Staatsrecht* (Hirzel, 1888), 1033. He

writes that *auctoritas* is "more than a piece of advice but less than an order" (*mehr als ein Rathschlag und weniger als ein Befehl*), 1034.

5. Dio Cassio 55.3. See also my discussion in "Authority: Some Fables," in *A World without Why* (Princeton University Press, 2014), 112–135.

6. The Greeks tended to confuse "Persians" and "Medes."

7. Obviously a further difficulty arises because we are actually speaking about the English word "authority," not the Latin *auctoritas*. This complicates things in a way I cannot discuss fully, but it does not invalidate the point I am trying to make. Full discussion of this matter would require treatment of passages like Matthew 8, where Jesus is speaking with a Roman centurion. The King James Version has the centurion say "I am a man under authority," where the Greek uses the word "ἐξουσία." One might think that the specifically Roman context here would predispose one to use the Latin word "*auctoritas*," but the Vulgate has "(*homo*) *sub potestate constitutus*" (Luther: "*der Obrigkeit untertan*"). "*Potestas*," however, is "ability, power." This strongly suggests that even in the late ancient world speakers of Latin did not think that "*auctoritas*" had the same nuance as "ἐξουσία." The same translation ἐξουσία/*potestas* (and not *auctoritas*) can be found in Matthew 7.28 (Luther: "*Vollmacht*"). The standard Catholic version (Douay-Rheims) has "authority" in the first of these passages and "power" in the second. The phantom appearance of "authority" in the English translations throws its shadow back onto these passages. This seems to me a good instance of the sort of thing Krigler was keen to train us to notice and avoid.

8. Plato, *Republic*, books 5, 6, and 7 (449–541).

9. Vladimir Lenin, *Staat und Revolution* (Laika, 2012), 108.

10. Thucydides 3.69–85.

11. Two particularly clear examples: Plutarch, *Themistocles* 21, and Plato, *Legg.* 722b.

chapter 4 Religion, Language, and History

1. I eventually wrote a paper on this in response to an invitation by Martin Bauer, translated as "Authority: Some Fables," in *A World without Why* (Princeton University Press, 2014), 112–135.

2. There is a completely different way of understanding and studying authority which one can find, for instance, in the writings of Alexandre

Kojève, who focused on the different ways in which humans can act on one another. "Authority" then designates various systematically asymmetrical modes of human interaction, of which Kojève distinguishes four main types. This is all done independently of the language actually used to describe these relations. Oddly enough, on this way of looking at things Krigler's view emerges as much closer to that of a language-centered analytic philosophy and of anarchism, while Kojève is, consciously, closer to Hegel in his method and his conclusions. Even if one prefers to follow Kojève, this would not in itself rehabilitate the literalist thesis about the absolute authority of the Bible. See Alexandre Kojève, *La notion de l'autorité* (Gallimard, 2008). This work was written in 1942, but not published until 2008, so Krigler would not have had access to it. *"L'autorité est la* possiblité *qu'a un agent d'agir sur les autres . . . sans que ces autres* réagissent *sur lui tout en étant* capables *de le faire,"* 58.

3. W. V. Quine, "Radical Translation," *Journal of Philosophy* 65 (1968): 200–201.

4. Krigler clearly used Adolph von Harnack's *Lehrbuch der Dogmengeschichte*, 3 vols. (Mohr, 1886, 1888, 1890) as a basic resource and quoted from it frequently.

5. The attentive reader will not fail to notice the obvious *tu quoque* arguments here concerning the use of, for instance, holy water in popular Catholicism, but also the central, and probably virtually indispensable, doctrine of transubstantiation. I never discovered what Krigler really thought about transubstantiation.

6. There was, Krigler said, a further theological dimension to all of this. God could use history, as it were, to send messages to later generations through the actions of people who were themselves completely unaware of what they were doing. This was the doctrine of "prefiguration." Isaac carrying the wood for the sacrifice on his back was a "prefiguration" of Christ's crucifixion, although Isaac did not know it, the people who originally transmitted the story did not know it, and the scribes who eventually put together the text of the book of Genesis did not know it. Only later could Christians look back on it and understand this aspect of what happened. So the writers' original intentions were not the last word in interpretations. For an introduction to the doctrine of prefiguration see Eric Auerbach, *Figura,* now in his *Scenes from the Drama of European Literature* (University of Minnesota Press, 1984); originally in *Neue Dantestudien* (n.p., 1944).

7. The basic synoptic book on canon formation is Jan Assmann's *Das kulturelle Gedächtnis* (Beck, 1997).

8. I once had the truly hair-raising experience of speaking to two Protestant missionaries who were translating "the Bible" (they meant the New Testament) into an African language which had a few hundred thousand speakers. This turned out to mean "translating" the text of the New English Bible into a "standard" language of their own invention for speakers of several related dialects.

9. This is one of the obvious implications of Heidegger's *Sein und Zeit* (Niemeyer, 1929).

10. See Ernst Bloch, *Thomas Münzer: Theologe der Revolution* (Aufbau, 1960).

11. John Dewey, *The Quest for Certainty* (1929); Theodor Adorno et al., *The Authoritarian Personality* (University of California Press, 1950).

12. Theodor Mommsen, *Römisches Staatsrecht* (Hirzel, 1888), 1022–1023. In general in his chapter on the competences of the Senate (vol. 3, part 2, 1022ff.), Mommsen hammers home the point that it had no power to act on its own. *"Er ist nichts als eine Verstärkung der Magistratur"* (The Senate is nothing but a body which strengthens the power of the magistrates). The real role of the Senate did, of course, evolve and develop over time. Here I am only referring to the slightly idealized conceptions that people had of its role during the late Republic.

13. Alison Cooley, *Res gestae divi Augusti* (Cambridge University Press, 2009), 58.

chapter 5   Human Variety

1. Paul Verlaine, *Oeuvres poétiques complètes*, Pléiade (Gallimard, 1962), 280.

2. See *Grundlegung zur Metaphysik der Sitten* (Riga, 1785), 30; also *Kritik der praktischen Vernunft* (Meiner, 1929), 96.

3. Søren Kierkegaard, *Fear and Trembling*, ed. Howard and Edna Hong (Princeton University Press, 1983).

4. György Lukács, *Geschichte und Klassenbewußtsein* (1923; Luchterhand, 1970).

5. Bernard Williams, "Moral Luck," in *Moral Luck and Other Essays* (Cambridge University Press, 1981).

6. In a way, of course, all of Christianity is organized around special dispensations, because that is exactly what Christian "grace" is supposed to be.

7. Wilhelm Weischedel, ed., *Immanuel Kant: Werkausgabe* (Suhrkamp, 1977), vol. 11, 53–61; see also Michel Foucault, "Qu'est-ce que les Lumières?" in *Dits et écrits IV: 1980–1988* (Gallimard, 1994), 562.

8. Horace *Epistulae* 1.2.40 (OCT).

9. MM §18.

10. MM §66.

11. I have often thought it is a great advantage of the system of education practiced at Cambridge and Oxford that at these institutions instruction is completely separated from examining. The supervisors (tutors, teachers) do not give grades; they are assigned by an independent board of examiners. This, in my experience, significantly detoxifies instruction, although, for a variety of complex reasons, it also tends to have a homogenizing effect on examining.

12. Bernard Williams, *Shame and Necessity* (University of California Press, 2008).

13. KSA 5.

14. The day after the Night of the Long Knives (30 June 1934), on which Hitler and the SS killed most of the leadership of the SA, Hitler had the whole German army assemble in their various barracks and swear an oath of fealty to him personally. Axel said that in his regiment one man had refused to swear, giving no reason for this other than that if this was a freely sworn oath then he was also free not to swear it. Axel then added that nothing had happened to this man. This was salt on Axel's wound, because it showed him that he himself originally really *could* have refused to swear the oath; in conversation he kept coming back to this point again and again.

15. I suppose with greater sophistication I might have seen this narrow focus on his oath as a kind of protective psychological displacement.

chapter 6   So, Liberal after All?

1. Hermann Schweppenhäuser and Rolf Tiedemann, eds., *Walter Benjamin: Gesammelte Werke* (Suhrkamp, 1991), vol. I/2, 690–708.

2. This might be another case in which one is tempted to cite Adorno's aphorism from MM §29: "*Der Splitter in Deinem Auge ist das beste Vergrößerungsglas.*"

chapter 7   Interlude: Nostalgia, a Trip to the City, Arrival

1. A. E. Housman, "Parody of a Greek Tragedy," originally in *The Bromsgrovian*, 1883.

2. The phrase "*ibis redibis non morieris in bello*" means either "You will go, you will return, you will not die in the war" or "You will go, you will not return, you will die in the war." To get the full effect requires the text to be unpunctuated, because the usual punctuation would have the effect of destroying the ambiguity, or the verse would have to be pronounced in a completely expressionless, unmodulated or chanting voice because otherwise the natural expressive grouping of the spoken words would give a clue to which meaning was intended. See also my "*Vix intelligitur*" in *A World without Why* (Princeton University Press, 2014).

3. Stefan Zweig, *Die Welt von Gestern* (Fischer, 1952).

4. Robert Musil, *Die Verwirrungen des Zöglings Törleß* (1906; Rowohlt, 1959).

chapter 8   Robert Paul Wolff: The Poverty of Liberalism

1. Robert Paul Wolff, *In Defense of Anarchism* (Harper & Row, 1970).

2. Johann Gottlieb Fichte, *Werke* (de Gruyter, 1971), vol. 3, 387–513.

3. Robert Paul Wolff, Herbert Marcuse, and Barrington Moore, *Kritik der reinen Toleranz* (Suhrkamp, 1965).

4. Michael Young, *The Rise of the Meritocracy: An Essay on Education and Equality* (Thames and Hudson, 1958).

5. For instance, in my *Philosophy and Real Politics* (Princeton University Press, 2008), 76ff.

6. See Hans-Georg Gadamer, *Wahrheit und Methode* (Mohr, 1960).

7. Robert Paul Wolff, *The Poverty of Liberalism* (Beacon, 1968).

8. John Rawls, *A Theory of Justice* (Harvard University Press, 1971)

9. MEW 1, 338ff.

10. Max Stirner, *Der Einzige und sein Eigentum* (1845; Reclam, 1972).

11. Stirner, *Der Einzige*, 5, 15.

12. Peter Kropotkin, *Mutual Aid: A Factor of Evolution* (1902; Freedom Press, 2009).

chapter 9   Sidney Morgenbesser: Philosophy as Practical Surrealism

1. Prof. X had been the youngest man to be awarded a degree by the university, the youngest person to have been named full professor, the youngest person elected to various professional and honorary societies— he himself tended to remind people of this. Sidney's comment: "He was the youngest person ever to have been born."
2. Kenneth J. Arrow, *Social Choice and Individual Values* (Wiley, 1951).
3. Robert Paul Wolff was very good on this issue, too, especially on the way in which the mono-dimensional Right-Left political spectrum was an artifact invented under the pressure of the need to justify a voting system that one had already adopted. The tail, that is, was wagging the dog. Wolff, a philosopher of many parts, also, by the way, gave excellent lectures on Kierkegaard.
4. If one says that in any of these cases the alternatives are not "irrelevant," then that just shows that "relevant/irrelevant" are too ill-defined for this schema to have any interesting application to reality.

chapter 10   Robert Denoon Cumming: Human Nature and History

1. *Human Nature and History: A Study of the Development of Liberal Political Thought,* 2 vols. (University of Chicago Press, 1969).

chapter 11   From Heidegger to Adorno

1. Werner Jaeger, *Paideia: Die Formung des griechischen Menschen* (de Gruyter, 1934–1947).
2. Werner Jaeger, *Early Christianity and Greek Paideia* (Harvard University Press, 1957). About twenty years later I was at the University of Chicago and got to know the philosopher Donald Davidson, who was also teaching there. Donald had been the roommate at Harvard of my doctoral supervisor, Bob Cumming, where both of them had studied classics as undergraduates. Donald was offered a fellowship to do a PhD with Jaeger. When he started to work he noticed that Jaeger kept talking about his own scholarly genealogy: his teacher, who his teacher's teacher had been, and so forth. He also seemed to mention rather more often than seemed appropriate that one or another of these, that is, of Jaeger's predecessors, had married the daughter of their teacher. At this point Jaeger would often invite his own daughter into

the room on some pretext or other. The daughter was perfectly charming, but Donald reported that he began to feel increasingly claustrophobic. Donald liked to be proactive and had a refreshing dose of cynicism in his makeup. For this reason he regularly (and consciously) over-recommended his own students. He once said to me about one of them that he would never do anything in philosophy, given that he was not that bright and also very indolent, but that he would give good dinner parties, and that was recommendation enough. At some level he really did believe that giving good dinner parties was as much of a recommendation for a university post as having thoughts about meaning and reference or the mind-body problem. (And, with increasing age, I have found myself less and less keen to disagree about this.) In matters of the heart he also preferred to have more control than it seemed was being envisaged for him by Jaeger. He eventually wrote a (very philological) dissertation on Plato's *Philebos* but not under Jaeger. The *diadoche* was broken.

3. In Paul Celan, *Lichtzwang* (Suhrkamp, 1970).

4. *Von Schwelle zu Schwelle* and *Mohn und Gedächtnis* were published in 1952 and 1955, respectively, by Deutsche Verlags-Anstalt. *Der Meridian und andere Prosa* was published in 1968 by Suhrkamp.

5. In a letter of 22 March 1962, Celan refers to his "*vieux coeur de communiste*," and in *Der Meridian* he says he "grew up" with the works of Kropotkin and Gustav Landauer: PCM, 44.

6. "*Himmel*" means either "sky" or "heaven." In the translation Celan made of this poem into French for his wife, he renders this as "*les bras envautourés par les ciels.*" See the commentary in *Paul Celan: Die Gedichte*, ed. Barbara Weidemann (Suhrkamp, 2018), 734. "*Ciel*" in French, however, has two different plurals: "*ciels*"= skies, and "*cieux*"= heavens. So the arms are vultured-around by skies, not heavens. Of course, no one simply reading the published text of this poem in 1967, as I was, could possibly have known this.

7. In fact, the word *Einhorn* (unicorn) turns out almost certainly to refer to a friend of Celan's named Erich Einhorn, but there was no way anyone simply reading the poems in 1967 could have known that. It is also the case that the poem is perfectly effective even if one does not know this. See Weidemann, ed., *Paul Celan*, 729.

8. PCM, 51.

9. PCM, 44.

10. PCM, 59.

11. PCM, 55.

12. PCM, 57.

13. PCM, 51.

14. PCM, 51–57.

15. PCM, 54.

16. Horace expresses the exclusionary intent in a famous passage (3.1): "*Odi profanum vulgus et arceo*" (I hate the common crowd and keep it at a distance).

17. On Stefan George and his circle, see Thomas Karlauf, *Stefan George: Die Entdeckung eines Charisma* (Blessing, 2007).

18. I got to know Gadamer only later in Heidelberg in 1971, when he was an *emeritus,* but still very much in evidence, although his preferred mode of action was pulling strings behind the scenes.

19. One of Celan's few works in prose, *Gespräch im Gebirg* (PCM, 23–29), is an imaginary conversation between Celan and Adorno, written after Celan failed, without explanation, to turn up for a planned meeting with Adorno in Switzerland.

20. Celan attempts to treat this complex of issues in greater detail are now accessible in the Tübingen edition of *Der Meridian,* ed. Bernhard Böschenstein and Heino Schmull (Suhrkamp, 1999).

21. Thomas Mann, *Die Entstehung des "Doktor Faustus": Roman eines Romans* (Fischer, 1984).

22. Theodor Wiesengrund Adorno, *Prismen: Kulturkritik und Gesellschaft* (Suhrkamp, 1955).

23. Theodor Wiesengrund Adorno, *Negative Dialektik* (Suhrkamp, 1966).

24. Ludwig Wittgenstein, *Philosophische Untersuchungen / Philosophical Investigations* (Blackwell, 1958).

25. Krigler, in particular, was of the party of Marcuse on this issue. He used to cite the saying of Jesus reported in some of the gospels about not putting new wine in old wineskins (Matthew 9.17), and he discussed the issue extensively when speaking of the incomprehension with which the Athenians received St. Paul's lecture on the Areopagos (*Praxeis* 17).

26. Theodor Wiesengrund Adorno et al., *Der Positivismusstreit in der deutschen Soziologie* (Luchterhand, 1969), 7–101.

27. MM §50; see also §5 & §44.

28. Krigler pointed out the potential circularity in the idea of *consensus omnium fidelium* because part of what made a person one of "the faithful" could be participation in the consensus.

chapter 12 Past, Present, Future

1. Theodor Wiesengrund Adorno, *Ästhetische Theorie* (Suhrkamp, 1970), 60–62. Most famously, perhaps, the Oulipo group tried to make arbitrarily adopted forms of *"contrainte"* an active principle of artistic creation. See Oulipo, *La littérature potentielle* (Gallimard, 1973). Thus, Georges Perec could write a whole novel, *La disparition* (Gallimard, 1969), without using the letter "e."

2. Bertolt Brecht, *Die Gedichte* (Suhrkamp, 1981), 744. Brecht seems to add to the strictly aesthetic a further political dimension, if one takes this passage together with that of another poem he wrote at about the same time:

   > *Was sind das für Zeiten, wo*
   > *ein Gespräch über Bäume fast ein Verbrechen ist*
   > *weil es ein Schweigen über so viele Untaten einschließt* (p. 723)

   What kind of times are they when / a conversation about trees is almost a crime / because it includes silence about so many atrocities

3. See also my "Nietzsche's Philosophical Ethnology," *Arion* 24, no. 3 (2017): 88–116.

4. I discuss "rights" more fully in *History and Illusion in Politics* (Cambridge University Press, 1999) and in "Human Rights: A Very Bad Idea" (with Lawrence Hamilton), *Theoria* 60 no. 135 (2013): 83–103.

5. See Andreas Malm, *Corona, Climate, Chronic Emergency: War Communism in the Twenty-First Century* (Verso, 2020).

6. Fabian Freyenhagen has recenty written a highly interesting paper on this: "Acting Irrespective of Hope," *Kantian Review* 25, no. 4 (2020): 605–630.

7. René Char, *Oeuvres complètes*, Pléiade (Gallimard, 1983), 208.

8. See my *Who Needs a World View?* (Harvard University Press, 2020), 55–82.

acknowledgments

I AM PARTICULARLY GRATEFUL TO Martin Bauer of *Mittelweg 36* for originally inviting me to write a short essay for the online journal *Soziopolis* about my first encounter with the thought of Karl Marx. I started writing about my old teacher Béla Krigler, about whom I hadn't really thought for decades. This turned out to open a floodgate of memories which now several years later has resulted in this text. Several other friends and colleagues, including Brian O'Connor, Lorna Finlayson, and Peter Garnsey, have discussed the topics treated here with me during the past few years, and I owe each of them a debt of gratitude. Hilary Gaskin read the whole text several times and gave it the benefit of her exacting judgment, and made numerous suggestions for improvements.

index

Picasso, Pablo, 101–102, 103, 147
plagiarism, 92–94
Plato, 49
pluralism, 95
political health, 156–157
politically acceptable alternative, 6–8
political philosophy, 49–51, 130
political theory, 139–140
politics, 1–2; aversion in, 163; concepts
    of variable aperture in, 94; fairness
    and equality not central to, 109–111;
    legislation not a good model of,
    109–111; legitimacy not central to,
    109–111, 119; as possibly based on
    liberalism, 24–26, 106–107, 165–167;
    as replacement of destiny, 14; as
    replacement of religion, 77; strategy
    in, 130
pope, the, 44–45; infallibility of,
    64–70
Portrait of the Artist as a Young Man
    (Joyce), 30
power: contrasted with authority,
    44–50; discrepancies of, 113
practices, social, 155–157
prejudice, 39–41, 127
pride, 41, 98
Prismen (Adorno), 152
prohibitions: canon of, 162; versus
    permissions, 121
property, 109–110, 120
Protestantism, 16, 83–84, 87–90, 138,
    158; Calvinist variant, 29, 31, 83–84,
    89; committed to isolated individual,
    35; as fetishistic, 58; Lutheran variant,
    56–65; motivated by need for simple
    answers to complex questions, 64,

77, 87; unable to tolerate uncertainty,
    66; views on revelation and inspi-
    ration, 76. *See also* conscience
prudence, 75, 79
psychoanalysis, 87–88
purity, 11, 41

Qur'an, 56

rational decision theory, 125–126
rationality, 15, 125
Rawls, John, 27, 117–119, 138, 143, 161
Reagan, Ronald, 139
reason: as concrete and contextual,
    not abstract and absolute, 39–41;
    distinguished from motivation,
    131–135; as guide, 65; not basis of
    ethics, 75–76
reciprocity, 121
redeeming the past, 93
refutation, 3–5, 9–10
religion, xiii, 3, 6, 8, 52, 72–78
remorse, 72
repentance, 72–74, 85
repression, 153–154, 157
Republic (Plato), 49
Res gestae divi Augusti, 69
Res novae, 69
responsibility, 87
results, 153, 157, 167
revelation, 56, 65, 76
revolution, 50, 91
rights, 129, 164
Rise of the Meritocracy, The (Young),
    114
Rosenberg, Julius and Ethel, exe-
    cution of, 104